Pen

nsylvania
RAILROAD

MIKE SCHAFER AND
BRIAN SOLOMON

MBI Publishing Company

First published in 1997 by MBI Publishing Company, PO Box 1, 729 Prospect Avenue, Osceola, WI 54020-0001 USA

MBI Publishing Company books are also available at discounts in bulk quantity for industrial or sales-promotional use. For details write to Special Sales Manager at Motorbooks International Wholesalers & Distributors, 729 Prospect Avenue, PO Box 1, Osceola, WI 54020-0001 USA.

Library of Congress Cataloging-in-Publication Data

Schafer, Mike.
    Pennsylvania Railroad / Mike Schafer and Brian Solomon.
        p. cm. --(Railroad color history)
        ISBN 0-7603-0379-7 (paperback : alk. paper)
    1. Pennsylvania Railroad. I. Solomon, Brian. II. Title. III. Series.
TF25.P4S33   1997
385'.09748--dc21   97-12593

COVER AND TITLE PAGE: Flagship of the mighty Pennsylvania Railroad from 1902 to the end of the PRR in 1968 was the world-class, all-Pullman *Broadway Limited*, shown striding out of Chicago behind a freshly washed trio of Electro-Motive E8 passenger diesels only moments following its long-traditional 5 p.m. departure from Chicago Union Station on a summer's late afternoon in 1965. At 9:30 a.m. the following morning, 907.7 miles and six states later, the *Broadway* will ease to a stop at Pennsylvania Station in Manhattan. *John Dziobko*

FRONTISPIECE: The nose of Pennsylvania Railroad GG1 No. 4800. This was the first of the famous G-class electric locomotive fleet that became synonymous with the PRR. The 4800 was built in 1934 and today resides that the Railroad Museum of Pennsylvania at Strasburg. *Brian Solomon*

BACK COVER: Two symbols of the Pennsylvania Railroad stand side by side at South Amboy, N.J., in 1954. At left is K4s-class Pacific-type steam locomotive No. 1361; at right, a classic GG1 electric clad in pin stripes. The K4s 4-6-2 locomotives were the Pennsy's signature steam power. This particular engine stood on display at Horseshoe Curve for nearly a quarter of a century after it was retired in the late 1950s. Early in the 1980s it was returned to operating condition for occasional excursion service. *John Dziobko*

Printed in China

CONTENTS

Acknowledgments

For its 121-year history, the Pennsylvania Railroad was a gargantuan, well-orchestrated effort that relied upon thousands upon thousands of visionaries, managers, and employees. This book was likewise a team effort, though not by thousands of team members. Not even hundreds. In fact, not even dozens.

But there certainly was more to the team than just the two names that appear as the book's authors. Even a book of this modest scope relies on the expertise of several individuals and even a couple of organizations and companies.

To start with, we must thank PRR expert Christopher T. Baer of the Hagley Museum and Library in Wilmington, Del. Chris' amazing abilities at helping us to interpret some of the PRR's complex history as well as that of America's in terms of commercial and transportation development as it related to PRR's evolution was invaluable.

PRR engineer at the throttle of J-class No.6445 at Gallitzin, Pa., in the mid-1950s. *Paul Brannen*

Another institution instrumental to this book project was the Railroad Museum of Pennsylvania at Strasburg. The Museum's George Deeming and Ken Riegel were most helpful in providing photo and resource material in a timely manner. The Railroad Museum of Pennsylvania is a showcase facility for those who would like a first-hand look at Pennsylvania Railroad equipment.

Many thanks must also go to Bill and Joann Caloroso. Bill, author of PENNSYLVANIA RAILROAD'S ELMIRA BRANCH (Andover Junction Publications, 1993), and his wife Joann welcomed us into their home for research expeditions. Bill offered his extensive PRR photo files as yet another source for some of this book's illustrative material. Similarly, we extend thank-yous to Dave and Jill Oroszi, who also generously opened their home and PRR photo collection to us and assisted with darkroom work.

To Steve Salamon in the great city of Pittsburgh, Pa., the heart of Pennsy country, we extend our appreciation for sharing his time (and several long-distance calls) in helping provide some of the hard-to-track-down information regarding PRR's extensive freight operations.

Much gratitude also must be showered on Andover Junction's Steve Esposito for his three weeks of intensive, almost nonstop research work. His understanding of business practices helped unravel at least a few of the numerous intricacies of early PRR development.

And finally, we would like to thank a host of other folks who in numerous different ways helped with the research, writing, editing, and/or production of this book: Mike Blaszak, Jack Consoli, Dan Cupper, John Dziobko, George Fletcher, Ron & Deb Goldfeder, John Gruber and son Richard, Tom Halterman, Richard J. Solomon, TTX Company's Bill Todd and Jim Pana, Chuck Yungkurth, Joseph Welsh, and, last but hardly least, the folks at Motorbooks International, particularly Jack Savage, Keith Mathiowetz, and Jana Solberg.

Introduction

So large and complex was the Pennsylvania Railroad, that one could write hundreds of books about the railroad and still not tell the whole story. In fact, hundreds of books, pamphlets and magazine articles *have* been written about the PRR. We're talking about a company that has long endured as one of the most revered rail institutions in U.S.—maybe even world—history.

There is absolutely no way a comprehensive history of the PRR can be covered in 128 pages and some 120 photos. Indeed, in 1993, a 96-page book was published that covered just *one branch* of the Pennsylvania Railroad (PENNSYLVANIA RAILROAD'S ELMIRA BRANCH, Bill Caloroso, Andover Junction Publications)!

To give readers an idea of the scope of this railroad consider this: The PRR itself commissioned the esteemed consulting firm of Coverdale & Colpitts to do a history of the railroad's first 100 years. The result was the CENTENNIAL HISTORY OF THE PENNSYLVANIA RAILROAD COMPANY, 1846-1946, published by the PRR in 1949. That text-heavy book (it has only 100 photos), which remains one of the authoritative treatises on the PRR, numbered 835 pages. That might seem more than sufficiently comprehensive to the lay railroad historian, yet hardcore PRR followers have been known to scoff at the work. Why? Because CENTENNIAL HISTORY OF THE PENNSYLVANIA RAILROAD is an abridged edition of the original submitted manuscript, which, had it been published in its entirety, would have numbered several thousand pages!

PRR public timetable from 1946 featured the railroad's famous T1 Duplex high-speed steam locomotive.

With these caveats, we introduce this first book in the Railroad Color History Series. We make no claim that this is the ultimate history of the Pennsylvania Railroad. Rather, this book serves as an historical overview and a handy reference source for basic matters relating to the PRR for the armchair transportation historian. The book illustrates how such a mighty railroad developed from humble, fragmented sources as well as how it operated as a system. The text and illustrations are meant to provide readers with a feel for the life and times of Pennsylvania Railroad and are not meant to document every aspect of PRR development and operations.

We do have a bonus, though. Knowing that railroad locomotives in particular hold great interest for the transportation audience, we have provided extra coverage of the PRR's vast locomotive fleet, with separate chapters for PRR steam, electric locomotives, and diesels. Arguably, the PRR had one of the most diverse and unusual locomotive armadas in all America.

If you find that this publication whets your appetite for more information about the Pennsylvania Railroad, then the book will have served one of its important goals. From here, there are numerous books, magazines, and other publications that readers can explore to find out more about the PRR and its many aspects. Check any of several railroad-enthusiast periodicals for ads regarding PRR-related books and videos.

This map of the Pennsylvania Railroad from a public timetable shows the railroad's width and breadth during its last full year of operation (1967); it will serve as a handy guide when reading about the construction of PRR's many varied routes. Though a few line segments had been abandoned by the time this map was rendered circa 1965, such as between Bay Head and Toms River, N.J., and that between Warren, Pa., and Olean, N.Y., most of the railroad was still intact.
Interestingly, although a number of connecting railroads are shown, rival New York Central's vital and very busy Chicago-Toledo-Cleveland-Buffalo main line has been completely (and conveniently) ignored, as has Baltimore & Ohio's main line between Chicago, Pittsburgh and Cumberland, Md.

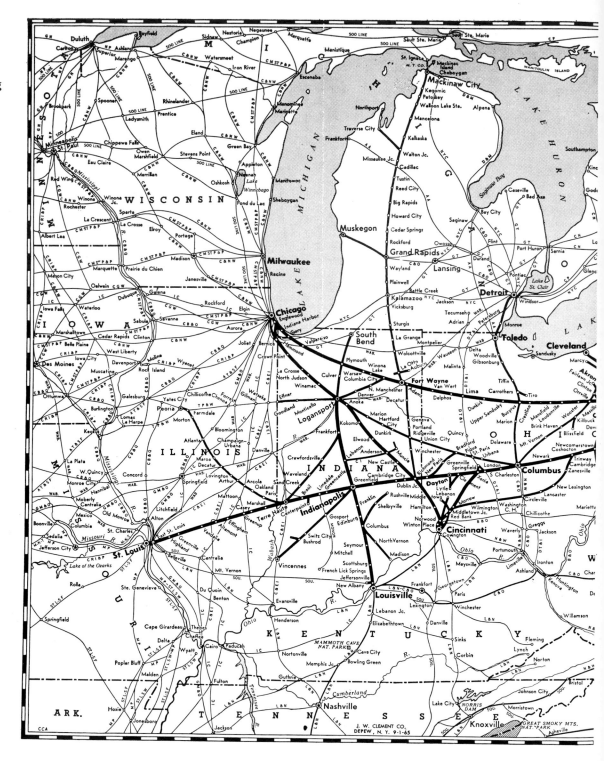

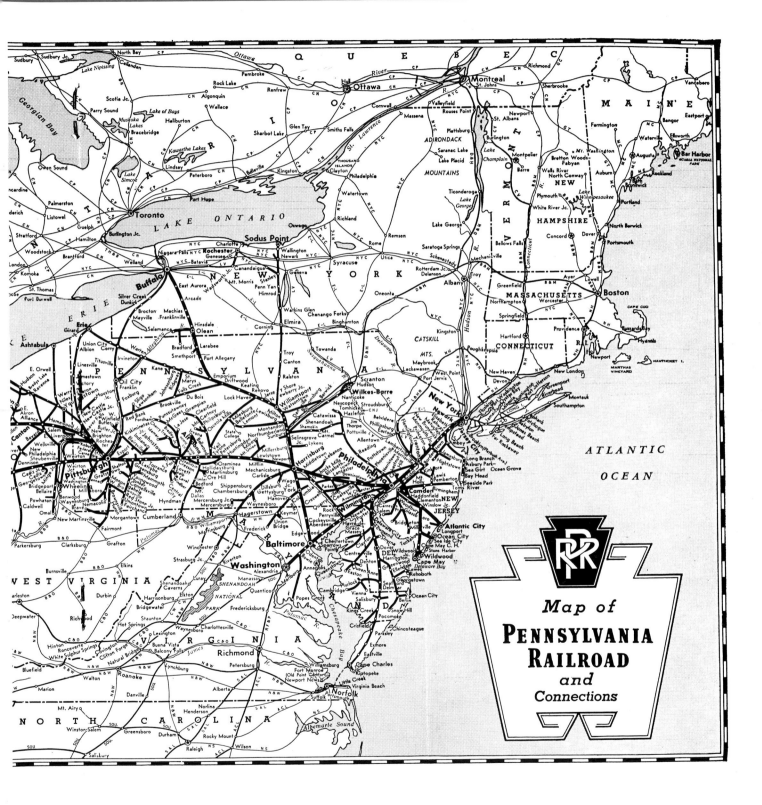

Map of
PENNSYLVANIA RAILROAD
and
Connections

9

The Pennsylvania Railroad's most recognizable landmark was its "World Famous Horseshoe Curve," shown here in a well-remembered 1952 painting by artist Grif Teller (1899-1993). Horseshoe was instrumental in allowing the railroad's Harrisburg-Pittsburgh Main Line to be built over the Allegheny Summit at a grade of less than 1.8 percent. The artist's perspective shows the curve as viewed southward from Kittanning Point; "artistic license" allows all four tracks to be seen directly in front, which in reality would have been difficult owing to the steepness of Kittanning Point—a viewer would have had to take life in hands to lean forward enough to see the northmost tracks almost straight below. The freight train at left, powered by a set of Baldwin-built "sharknose" freight diesels, is climbing toward the summit at Gallitzin, Pa., while a New York-bound passenger train behind a set of Electro-Motive (General Motors) diesels cruises down toward Altoona at the base of the mountains as a steam-powered freight in the distance also drifts downgrade. Cradled in the valley of the Curve is the City of Altoona reservoir. The flag and the little stone building denote the location of Horseshoe Curve Park, which in recent years has become a popular, well-developed tourist attraction.

Dawn of the Pennsylvania Railroad

BIRTH OF A DYNASTY

At the opening of the nineteenth century, the United States comprised 17 disparate states, most of which were strung out along the Atlantic seaboard. The commerce of this fragile Union centered around the likes of Boston, New York, Philadelphia and Washington, D.C. To the west lay a wall of mountains—the Appalachians—forming a formidable barrier to the vast, largely unsettled frontier beyond.

The Union was pretty evenly divided as to how it viewed the world beyond the mountains—lands which included the territories of Ohio, Kentucky, Tennessee and the newly purchased Louisiana Territory. On one hand you had the folks who were perfectly content in making the existing 17 states work as a unified country, and on the other you had the visionaries who saw the "American West" as ripe for farming and other development.

Some feared that any extensive degree of migration to the West would diminish the existing Union. Still others felt that any large-scale settlement in the West would simply lead to the formation of a separate country owing to the barrier that was the Appalachians, precluding any chance of a truly unified United States.

Regardless, there was no stopping westward destinies. Settlers flowed into the new territories unabated, thanks in part to roads, some of which had been established as early as the second half of the eighteenth century including at least one that had been funded by the State of Pennsylvania in the 1790s.

Commerce in those times moved by water and road. Generally, bulk goods like grain and flour descended inland rivers to New Orleans where they were either exported or shipped to Atlantic seaboard ports like New York and Philadelphia. The return trade, which was largely light goods (textiles, hardware, and such) imported from Europe or manufactured in Eastern cities, was carried in relatively small lots over land. Livestock tended to move east on the roads, while coal and ore were moved in both directions via wagons and pack horses.

In 1806, Congress authorized construction of the National Road—paved with gravel—from Cumberland, Md., to Ohio Territory via what is now Wheeling, W. Va.; its construction would take more than a quarter of a century. The National Road provided a commercial artery to the West for both Baltimore and Washington.

Canals were becoming a popular means of transport as the nineteenth century got under way, although they were sometimes hampered by mountains. Canals served as extensions to navigable waterways as well as links between cities.

And what of railways? What were *they*? In the minds of Americans of that period, railways were largely horse-powered curiosities born in England to serve coal mines, although the concept of rail as a viable alternative to roads and canal was

An express passenger train out of Harrisburg bound for Philadelphia is scooping water "on the fly" (at speed) at Radnor, one of Philadelphia's many suburban communities. A high-stepping Atlantic-type locomotive (4 pilot wheels, 4 driving wheels, 2 trailing wheels; thus a "4-4-2") leads the five-car train in this 1906 view of PRR's "Main Line" route, as its line between Philadelphia and Pittsburgh was known. *Cal's Classics*

Between Philadelphia and Harrisburg, the Main Line passes through an agricultural side of Pennsylvania geography, farmed by Amish. Twin GG1 electrics have the westbound *Manhattan Limited* in tow en route from New York to Chicago during a spring day in 1967. The G's will be replaced by diesel power at Harrisburg. *John Dziobko*

beginning to take hold on American soil in isolated applications.

The years 1807 and 1817 were both watersheds for American transportation. In 1807 Robert Fulton introduced the steamboat, which overnight propelled water transport into a new era. And in 1817—when the first U.S. common-carrier railway was still a decade away—construction began on one of the most-significant waterways of the nineteenth century: the 363-mile Erie Canal, connecting the Hudson River with the eastern end of Lake Erie.

Transportation development during the first two decades or so of the nineteenth century was an on-again, off-again proposition, thanks to the War of 1812 (which lasted until 1815) and the postwar depression of 1819-1822. Stymied about what to do for better transportation to the West was the State of Pennsylvania and its

anchor city, Philadelphia. With the abuilding National Road to the south and the likewise under-construction Erie Canal to the north, many Philadelphians saw possible ruin for their city as inland trade and travel was siphoned away through the rival cities of New York and Baltimore. Concerned citizens rallied that Philadelphia and Pennsylvania interests must sponsor a new transportation artery to the West, the looming 2,300-foot-high Allegheny Mountain range notwithstanding. Unfortunately, then—as now—politics impeded progress. Although several bills were put forth proposing various plans for a new east-west transportation corridor, they were continuously stalemated by squabbling special interest groups.

Things came to a head in 1824 when the Chesapeake & Ohio Canal, being built westward along the Potomac River to serve Washington and, later, Baltimore, became the object of possible federal aid. This broke the political stalemates within the Pennsylvania legislature, and state officials soon authorized surveys for a canal system linking Harrisburg and Pittsburgh. The state commissioners did the survey work themselves and in 1825 recommended that a trans-state canal be constructed, "crossing" the Allegheny ridge via a four-mile tunnel under same.

Meanwhile, a gala event was taking place nearly 200 miles north as the Erie Canal officially opened on October 26, 1825. The fanfare would be deserved. Not only would the Erie Canal help colonize western New York, but its impact eventually would be felt throughout the Great

LEFT: Strategically located on the Susquehanna River, Harrisburg prospered to become the state capital—and a vital hub for the Pennsylvania Railroad. As was befitting an important PRR city, the railroad in 1887 erected a rambling red brick and granite Victorian passenger depot adjacent to the south side of the business district near the state capitol building. In the 1980s, the building underwent extensive restoration for its continued duties as a transportation gateway for Harrisburg. *Mike Schafer*

BELOW: Rockville Bridge across the Susquehanna a short distance north of Harrisburg was opened to traffic in 1902. It is the longest stone-arch railroad bridge in the world. In this scene dating from November 1956, a 104-car freight led by an M-class Mountain strides west across the 3,820-foot bridge. The tracks in the foreground of this eastward view swing north and west to Pittsburgh. At left across the river Is another steam-powered freight coming off the line from Buffalo. *Robert Malinoski*

Lakes west of Lake Ontario, particularly in the development of the new lake-hugging commercial centers of Buffalo, Cleveland and Chicago.

Another development that same year drew considerably less notice: John Stevens built and demonstrated a steam locomotive on a circle of track at Hoboken, N.J. He had perhaps taken a cue from a number of rudimentary steam locomotives that had been built in England as early as 1804—including George Stephenson's first engine in 1814.

Stevens was a visionary who was persistent in his views that rail transport would be superior to canals and roads, and he had a particular interest in steam power regardless of what it was propelling. This same man had, in 1815, received a charter to build a railroad between Trenton and New Brunswick, N.J., but the project died for lack of interest. Interestingly, Stevens in

1823, proposed construction of a "Pennsylvania Rail Road" between Philadelphia and Columbia, Pa., on the Susquehanna River a few miles southeast of Harrisburg (also on the Susquehanna), but the scheme fell through—temporarily.

The Main Line of Public Works

On February 25, 1826, the Pennsylvania state legislature officially authorized construction of a Harrisburg-Pittsburgh canal—the Pennsylvania Canal. On July 4 of that year, work began on two of the canal's segments, one on each side of the Alleghenies. Also in 1826, the Philadelphia, Lancaster & Columbia Rail Road was incorporated to do exactly what John Stevens had proposed three years earlier: connect the Quaker City with Columbia. Although canals were in high vogue, the lack of an adequate source of water between Philadelphia and Columbia provided further impetus to actually build the PL&C. Surveys were laid for the final location of the railroad, but construction would not begin until 1829.

In 1826, the Mohawk & Hudson became the first chartered U.S. railroad to actually be built, and in 1827 the nation's first com-

Westbound out of Harrisburg's Enola Yard, freight M-9 led by 4-8-2 No. 6744 storms along the Susquehanna River on August 22, 1956. A short distance away at Duncannon, confluence of the Juniata River and the Susquehanna, the Main Line will veer west to follow the former almost to Altoona. *Robert Malinoski*

mon-carrier railway was chartered, the Baltimore & Ohio Railroad. As its named implied, the B&O was headed west, and it would prove critical in the birth of the Pennsylvania Railroad. For the State of Pennsylvania, 1827 represented just another setback in its transportation quests when it was concluded that the all-canal route then under construction between the Susquehanna River and Pittsburgh would be impractical, though a combination of canal and railway might hold promise.

In 1828 the state unveiled revised plans for its Philadelphia-Pittsburgh transportation artery, heretofore the Pennsylvania Canal. Under the name of Main Line of Public Works, the state would cobble together a system of conveyances to move passengers and freight, although exactly which type and combination of conveyances—canal, railway, turnpike, and perhaps even inclined planes (for mountain crossing)—was subject to controversy.

Construction of the canal portions had been continuous since 1826; in March 1831, the state authorized the construction of railways (or in some cases the inclusion of ones already under way) to interlink the canals. The integrated 395-mile-long system that finally emerged comprised (com-

Double-headed steam locomotives tromp along the four-track Main Line near Altoona with a long limited—possibly the New York-Columbus-Chicago *Metropolitan*—in the summer of 1929. *Cal's Classics*

BELOW: The Altoona shop complex appears pristine in this westerly view from about 1910. *Railroad Museum of Pennsylvania*

pletion date in parenthesis), east to west, a railroad—the Philadelphia & Columbia, which had evolved from the PL&C mentioned earlier—between Broad Street in Philadelphia and Columbia, 82 miles (1834); the Pennsylvania Canal along the Susquehanna and Juniata (JOO-nee-attah) rivers between Columbia and Hollidaysburg, 172 miles (1832); an incline plane railway over the Allegheny summit—the Allegheny Portage Railroad—between Hollidaysburg and Johnstown, 36 miles (1834); and another waterway, the Western Division Canal, along the Conemaugh, Kiskiminetas, and Allegheny rivers, between Johnstown and Pittsburgh, 104 miles (1830). The system included several branch canals.

The P&C was in fact the first rail line built of what would become the sprawling Pennsylvania Railroad empire. When P&C's first segments opened in 1832, passengers rode in horse-drawn cars, and parts of the railroad were operated as inclined planes. The P&C opened in its entirety on October 7, 1834, with the dispatch of two special trains, one carrying the governor of Pennsylvania and each powered by a steam locomotive—the *Lancaster* and the *Columbia* respectively—both built by Baldwin Locomotives Works.

Although the Main Line of Public Works was not completed until 1834, several years after the Erie Canal and the National Road/C&O Canal had been operating (and indeed had diverted traffic from Philadelphia ports), it managed to garner much business. A trip across the state which previously could have taken up to 20 days now took less than five. All was not perfect, though. The trip involved annoying and time-consuming changes between transport modes; further, between mid-December and mid-March virtually the whole system was shut down account of the canals freezing over.

The engine terminal at East Altoona in 1955 reveals PRR steam in sunlight—but also in twilight, as PRR steam was in the midst of being phased out. At left, a 2-10-4 of Pennsy's J class shares the sunlight with a diesel invader, in this case a set of Baldwin shark freight diesels. PRR's brutish Texas-type steam engines, as illustrated by the 6432 taking on water in this scene, were used primarily west of Altoona where it was at home lugging tonnage up around Horseshoe Curve to the summit of the Alleghenies as well as along the relatively low-grade route beyond to Pittsburgh. *John Dziobko*

The Allegheny Portage portion of the trip was particularly ingenious. Westbound, at the Hollidaysburg transfer point, passengers either changed from canal boat to an APRR train, or, if they were riding on special sectional canal packet boats, they simply stayed aboard the packet as it was placed aboard a special railcar. APRR trains moved by mule or horse power along segments of level tracks linking a series of ten inclined planes, each a half mile or less long. To traverse the incline sections, the railcars were unhitched from animal power, attached to heavy ropes or cables, and drawn up or eased down the inclines via stationary steam engines. Eventually the animal power was replaced by steam locomotives, and another day was lopped from the cross-state trip.

The Main Line of Public Works was the engineering wonder of its day, but destined to be short-lived (although the APRR segment was around long enough to host a famous writer and novelist, Charles Dickens, and the bodies of two presidents, William Henry Harrison in 1841 and Zachary Taylor in 1850). In the end, it became apparent that the Main Line project had been unwisely handled by the State, principally because of the enormous debt that had been incurred building branch canals. Then, in the middle of a serious depression that lasted from 1839 to 1843, the State defaulted on its interest payments and curtailed public works projects.

This scenario, coupled to the ongoing B&O threat, caused Philadelphians to begin pushing for a privately operated all-rail artery across Pennsylvania. Part of the groundwork for this had already been done. In 1839-40, engineer Charles Lyon Schlatter had mapped out alignments for an all-rail route between Harrisburg and Pittsburgh. Schlatter narrowed his surveys to three options: a so-called Northern Route via today's Williamsport, surmounting the Allegheny ridge southeast of where today's Interstate 80 crosses near Snow Shoe; a Southern Route which roughly follows today's Pennsylvania Turnpike; and a Middle Route—which Schlatter thought to be the best—along the Susquehanna and Juniata rivers.

Birth of the Pennsylvania Railroad

Booming Pittsburgh was pivotal to the birth of what was to become one of America's most-influential railroad dynasties. Strategically located at the juncture of the Allegheny and Monongahela rivers, which formed the Ohio River, Pittsburgh was fast becoming an industrial center and transportation hub. When the Baltimore & Ohio announced it was heading for Pittsburgh and in 1843 requested charter for a line to do just that, city fathers and merchants opened their arms. They knew that the railway would be a faster and cheaper means of moving goods (and people) to and from Eastern markets and ports—and they didn't care if those ports were Baltimore's.

This alarmed Philadelphians, of course. In 1844 the state legislature became involved, and in 1845 a proposal was put forth for a through railroad. In 1846 two

bills were introduced. One authorized the B&O to build that railroad while the second proposed a "Pennsylvania Central Railroad" to do the job. On March 19, 1846, the state House passed a bill for a "Pennsylvania Railroad"; on March 26, the Senate did likewise. On April 13, 1846, the charter for The Pennsylvania Railroad Company was signed by the Governor to authorize construction of a railroad from Harrisburg to Pittsburgh. Welcome to the world, PRR.

Despite the new railroad, B&O was still in the running for Pittsburgh, and as to which of the two railroads would finally lay claim to that city became a highly controversial issue. The B&O was already well under way, having reached Cumberland, Md., 178 miles out of Baltimore, while the PRR was for all practical purposes still only electrons in the minds of its backers—although a rail system was indeed already up and running between Philadelphia and Harrisburg thanks to the MLofPW's Philadelphia & Columbia and the Harrisburg, Portsmouth, Mount Joy & Lancaster railroads.

Fortunately, the PRR had ardent supporters—many of them Philadelphia merchants and city fathers, of course—and by one vote they altered a bill in the legislature that would have authorized the B&O to be the dominating railroad in Pittsburgh. Of course, that was but a fraction of the battle that lay ahead. The PRR at this point really only existed as a lofty proposal, and the altered bill required that certain caveats, such as construction and stock issuance, be met by certain dates or the plan would default, allowing the B&O to become the kingpin railroad of Pittsburgh.

The Main Line across Pennsylvania

John Edgar Thomson was named chief engineer of the new Pennsylvania Railroad on April 9, 1847. The 39-year-old's first task was to select one of the three routes surveyed by George Schlatter several years earlier. Thomson concluded what Schlatter had felt: that the Middle Route overall showed the best potential.

CHAPTER 1

This route followed the Susquehanna River west from Harrisburg to the mouth of the Juniata River near what is today Duncannon, Pa. From there, the alignment hugged the Juniata to Lewistown. Because railroads of the period tended to favor low grades, Schlatter had proposed a long, steady climb toward the summit that began in the vicinity of today's Lewistown, leaving the banks of the Juniata River at that point. The route cut across Jacks Mountain and veered southwesterly along the shoulders of the Kishacoquillas Valley until it again reached the Juniata River valley at Mill Creek. From there, the route—all the while still climbing along valley shoulders—followed the Juniata and Little Juniata rivers until it became grafted onto the east slopes of Allegheny Mountain. Climbing southwesterly along the east slopes of Allegheny Mountain, it reached the summit at Sugar Gap, near today's

Gallitzin. Once the Allegheny spine was surmounted, the sailing was relatively easy all the way to Pittsburgh over the more-gentle terrain of the Allegheny Plateau.

Construction on the new PRR's Eastern Division began at Harrisburg in 1847 and the railroad was opened for business as far west as Lewistown in 1849. At Lewistown, Thomson deviated from the Schlatter survey simply by staying at water level with the Juniata River rather than begin a long climb to Sugar Gap; the river-level route was longer but eliminated long, though gradual, grades. Construction reached Huntingdon by June the following year. At Tyrone, Thomson veered southward along the Little Juniata River to a swampy area destined to become Altoona, and then continued beyond to Duncansville, located on the Main Line of Public Works.

By the start of October 1850, the entire line between Harrisburg and a connection

Westbound freight NWC-1 bound from Greenville Yard (Jersey City) to Conway Yard in Pittsburgh grinds up around the north swing of Horseshoe Curve on a lush June afternoon in 1965. Though now off limits to photographers, this vantage point is very near that which is depicted in the Grif Teller painting that leads this chapter. *Robert Malinoski*

DAWN OF THE PENNSYLVANIA RAILROAD

Awash in autumn splendor, the heart of Horseshoe Curve is illustrated in this northward view taken from the mountainside that forms the south wall of the valley of Burgoon Run. The two diesels leading a downbound coal train are backdropped by the stone face of Kittanning Point. Plainly visible to the right of the diesels is then-retired Class K4s steam locomotive 1361 serving as the centerpiece for Horseshoe Curve Park. The park's canteen and gift shop is at parking-lot level below. Many first-time visitors to Horseshoe are surprised to learn that the curve is perched halfway up the mountainside, and that to see the trains pass, one must make a hefty stair climb (or ride the park's new incline railway) to the trackside "plateau" of the park. *Mike Schafer*

with the east end of the Allegheny Portage Railroad at Duncansville opened for service. The connection with the APRR together with PRR's newly acquired (1848) control of the Harrisburg, Portsmouth, Mount Joy & Lancaster meant that it was now possible to travel by rail (albeit with a train change or two) all the way from Philadelphia to Johnstown. State-owned tracks were still used between Dillersville, the connection with the HPMtJ&L near Lancaster, and Philadelphia; canal travel was still necessary west from Johnstown.

Meanwhile, in May 1850, the State had decided that a standard railroad route over the summit would be feasible and commenced building the 41-mile New Portage Railroad to replace the incline-plane sections of the APRR. The line was not completed until 1856, although that is getting ahead of the story a mite.

Construction of PRR's Western Division between Pittsburgh and Johnstown was less speedy than construction east of the mountains. By late summer 1851, construction had reached east from Pittsburgh to a point 21 miles west of Johnstown. Not until almost the end of 1852 were the remaining 28 miles to Cresson (near Gallitzin) completed. Here again, Thomson deviated from Schlatter's plan, following the Conemaugh River from the connection with the Portage Railroad near Cresson through Johnstown to a point near Blairsville before striking south and west through what is today Latrobe and Greensburg to Pittsburgh— an alignment that lay south of Schlatter's Middle Route survey.

But when the Western Division was finished, one finally could cross the state on an all-rail route. On December 10, 1852, the first through train left Philadelphia for Pittsburgh. The nemesis of this first all-rail route, though, was what had once been hailed as an engineering breakthrough: the incline-plane segment. The APRR's plane-and-cable system was cumbersome, and the PRR had to pay tolls to the State wherever PRR trains had to use MLofPW facilities, such as between Philadelphia and Lancaster and Duncansville and Cresson.

Thomson had known that the APRR link was but a stopgap measure if backers of the PRR were truly serious about it being truly competitive with the B&O and yet

ABOVE: The engine crew of this Class L 2-8-2 appear to be as interested in the group of photographers as the photographers are in capturing the crew's engine, the 1487, slugging through Horseshoe Curve on November 20, 1947. RIGHT: Nearly all freights making the westbound climb out of Altoona were (and still are) assisted by a set of helper locomotives pushing at the hind end of the train. On this day in July 1948, no less than three locomotives—two of them running in reverse— help a freight achieve the summit. *Both photos, Bruce D. Fales, Jay Williams Collection*

22

another growing threat, the Erie Railroad across New York's Southern Tier, both of which were busy completing their main lines into the West. In fact, work had already started, in 1851, on what would be PRR's Mountain Division, designed to link its Eastern and Western divisions with a new route over the Allegheny summit.

Lack of money hampered progress on the Mountain Division, and Thomson's pleas to raise capital fell deaf upon the conservative ears of PRR President W. C. Patterson. The state was dragging its heels as well, becoming fully aware that if the Mountain Division were a success, both the state's APRR and the New Portage line—indeed the whole Main Line of Public Works—would be rendered a lame duck.

Three bores carried the PRR Main Line under the topmost ridge of the Alleghenies' spine at the town of Gallitzin. This eastward view from a street overpass in Gallitzin in this scene from circa 1967 shows two of the bores. At left is Gallitzin Tunnel while the westbound ore train is emerging from Allegheny Tunnel. Opened in 1854, Allegheny Tunnel was the first of the three bores that would carry rail traffic under the ridge. If you were to climb the steeple of the church in the background, you'd be able to see westbound trains approaching the tunnels in the valley on the other side of the ridge. The EMD locomotives in this scene are being used as mid-train helpers, ore being a particularly heavy commodity to hoist up grades. Even with the mid-train locomotives, a set of helpers was still necessary at the hind end. *Jim Boyd*

LEFT: New Portage Tunnel, located a short distance south and east of the bores shown on the previous page, was built by the state-owned New Portage Railroad as part of that company's valiant effort to open its own all-rail route over the Alleghenies. The tunnel's west portal is shown not long after the bore was opened in 1855. Although the PRR acquired and then temporarily abandoned most of the NPRR, New Portage Tunnel came to be used primarily for eastbound PRR traffic headed down the mountain while nearby Allegheny and Gallitzin tunnels were reserved mainly for westbound traffic. *Railroad Museum of Pennsylvania*   BELOW: Bucking conventional traffic patterns, a westbound PRR freight emerges from New Portage Tunnel in 1966. By this time, PRR had single-tracked the tunnel so that larger freight cars could be accommodated. Using a telephoto lens, the photographer was standing approximately at the location of the depot in the earlier view. *Jim Boyd*

CHAPTER I

The manner in which Thomson solved the problem demonstrated his resolve—not to mention his visionary leadership capabilities: Thomson got himself elected as the new president of the Pennsylvania Railroad in 1852.

Once in that esteemed position, the PRR marched boldly into the annals of U.S. railroad history. Thomson's first major concern as president was to complete the Mountain Division. His first step was to float bond issues, and in doing so, Thomson and PRR stockholders raised $3 million in September 1852.

The Mountain Division Becomes Reality

In the overall network of what became the showcase Pennsylvania Railroad of the twentieth century, the original Mountain Division was a relatively short stretch of railway—less than 40 miles. But it was such a pivotal endeavor to the future of the PRR and an engineering masterpiece that it deserves a special highlight as the pinnacle of this first chapter of Pennsy history.

So remarkable was this stretch of line (specifically, the 14.4-mile climb from Altoona around Horseshoe Curve to Cresson, Pa.) that it currently enjoys the status of national historic landmark—one that still draws tourists from all over the world.

Thomson's concept on how to sur-

mount the summit of the Alleghenies was brilliant. Although Thomson overall had followed Schlatter's Middle Route alignment from Harrisburg to Pittsburgh, we have already noted that Thomson's main deviation occurred west of Lewistown, beyond which he maintained a water-level route some 70 miles west and southwestward through today's Altoona to the APRR at Duncansville.

Although the line had been continued this way in part to reach the APRR, it was Thomson's intention that the Altoona site would be the staging point for the PRR's future attack on the summit. From here, the summit could be achieved with a moderately steep grade in a relatively short distance. Helper engines would be required to assist in hoisting trains over the summit, but the helper district would be relatively concentrated. Nourished with the new bond monies, construction of the Mountain Division resumed in 1852.

The plan dictated that the line up to the summit, which would cling on the valley walls of various "runs" (streams) and in some locations simply cut through low ridges, could not exceed a grade of 1.8 percent (that is, a rise of 1.8 feet in 100 linear feet), and indeed the builders were able to keep it at 1.75 percent or less on most portions of the climb. But construction was stymied at one location about five and a half miles out of Altoona where the valley of

Johnstown, Pa., will probably forever be best known for the devastating flood that wiped out many of its inhabitants as well as much of the PRR in 1889. Almost 70 years later, in 1958, things appear considerably drier as the eastbound *Pennsylvania Limited* snakes through Johnstown en route from Chicago to New York. Nearby concrete walls attest to water control projects undertaken since the deluge to prevent it from happening again. *Richard J. Solomon*

A postcard view of Union Station in Pittsburgh, circa 1910. This was the fifth station that the PRR occupied in downtown Pittsburgh and the fourth Union Station. It was located at the convergence of the original Pennsylvania Railroad, the Pittsburgh, Fort Wayne & Chicago and the Panhandle, hence the "union station" designation. This view looks northeast. At left, crossing over Liberty Street, is the PFtW&C approach tracks and US Tower. The Panhandle tracks lie between the depot building and the powerhouse at right. The PRR approached the station from behind, where a portion of the station's original arch train shed is visible. The depot building today serves as "The Pennsylvanian" apartments and looks surprisingly the same, having been carefully rehabbed. The station's signature rotunda has been declared an historic landmark. Amtrak passenger trains still pause here, but passengers use a new facility that has been grafted onto the north side of the depot building at street level. *Collection of Steve Salamon*

Burgoon Run, which the line was following, abruptly ended at a mountainside promontory—Kittanning Point.

To shortcut across the valley to gain access to the ridge that builders wanted the track to use to reach the summit would have meant a short (just over one mile) but intolerably steep (almost 4½ percent) grade. Thomson's answer was to slice the face off Kittanning Point, take the line down to the end of the valley, and circle it across Kittanning Point on fills that spanned the ravines of Kittanning Run and Glen White Run on either side. This huge semi-circle of iron became known as Horseshoe Curve.

This little side trip to Kittanning Point added almost two miles to the run, but it enabled builders to honor the maximum gradient of 1.8 percent—in fact, they bettered it at 1.75 percent, and on the tightest point of Horseshoe Curve itself the grade was held at 1.45 percent, in part to compensate for the tightness of the curve.

The railroad tunneled the summit ridge, about five miles up from Horseshoe, through a bore named Allegheny Tunnel at what is today Gallitzin. From there it was an easy downgrade along the Allegheny Plateau to Johnstown and the connection with the Western Division. The tunnel eliminated an additional 150 feet of climbing.

Horseshoe Curve's opening on February 15, 1854, was followed by a (predicted) boom in traffic and development along the Harrisburg-Pittsburgh route—and the overnight near death of APRR's nearby incline-plane system. Travel time between those two points could now be accomplished in as little as 13 hours, and by the end of 1852 the route between Altoona—the new town that had been established by the railroad at the base of the climb—and Conemaugh had been double-tracked to handle the volume of business.

Initially a setback in the construction of PRR's Mountain Division, "The Curve" was now hailed as the new engineering triumph. To ship and travel via the "Horseshoe Curve Route" was to choose the preferred all-rail routing between East and West. The B&O and Erie had been relegated to secondary status, and Pittsburgh was about to become very much a PRR city.

In the middle of all this, the State inexplicably trudged on with its building of the New Portage Railroad to replace the incline-plane APRR segment of the Main Line of Public Works. The NPRR opened by 1856, complete with its own mini-version of Horseshoe—Muleshoe Curve—and its own 2,000-foot tunnel under the summit ridge called New Portage Tunnel. The

CHAPTER I

effort was much in vain, for the MLofPW route still relied in part on canals. People and shippers wanted speed, which was exactly what the PRR offered. In 1857, the state put the Main Line of Public Works up for sale.

PRR became the purchaser of the MLof-PW that same year and subsequently the new owner of the (now toll-free) Philadelphia & Columbia and New Portage railroads. PRR now had its own route east all the way to Philadelphia plus a secondary line over the summit of the Alleghenies—although the PRR abandoned the New Portage line almost immediately, transferring its rails to the Pittsburgh, Fort Wayne & Chicago, which was building between those namesakes—and which is a principal player in the chapter that follows.

Pittsburgh was the west-end anchor of the Pennsylvania's Main Line, and it became a critically important city for the PRR. The city's downtown provides an impressive backdrop in another memorable Grif Teller painting entitled "Pittsburgh Promotes Progress," commissioned by the Pennsylvania Railroad for its 1954 calendar. The view looks northeast from the confluence of the Allegheny (left) and the Monongahela (right) rivers. The tugboat is at the very beginning of the Ohio River. The painting shows an Ohio-bound Panhandle passenger that has just left downtown, having crossed the Monongahela on the Panhandle Bridge, which would be out of the scene at right in the distance. The two roadway spans shown are the Manchester Bridge (left) and the Point Bridge. The grassy area at the end of those two bridges was the site of Fort Duquesne and later the location of PRR's Duquesne Freight Station; once the railroad facilities were cleared away after World War II, it became Point State Park as shown here. Artist Teller was commissioned by the PRR for a number of illustrations, used on calendars, timetables, and other Pennsy promotional material.

The Pennsylvania Railroad was a major player in Chicago and several other large Midwestern urban centers notably St. Louis, Indianapolis, and Cincinnati. Chicago was one of the railroad's two principal connecting points (the other being St. Louis) with railroads that reached into the American West. "Home" for PRR passenger trains at Chicago was Chicago Union Station. On a hazy summer morning in June 1967, PRR's *South Wind* has just departed CUS on its 1,559-mile journey to Miami, Fla. Jointly operated with Louisville & Nashville, Atlantic Coast Line, and Seaboard Air Line, the *South Wind* will traverse PRR rails through Logansport and Indianapolis to Louisville where it will be handed over to L&N. *Mike Schafer*

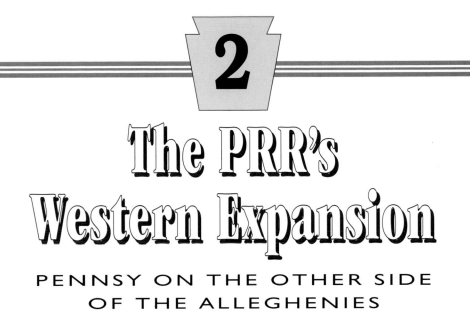

The PRR's Western Expansion

PENNSY ON THE OTHER SIDE OF THE ALLEGHENIES

As Pennsylvania Railroad President J. Edgar Thomson was pushing his railroad along to Pittsburgh in the mid-1800s, work was already under way west of there to expand PRR's reach.

The PFTW&C and Associated Lines

The Ohio & Pennsylvania, first projected by Philadelphians in 1848, was being built to connect Pittsburgh with Crestline, Ohio, while the Ohio & Indiana would connect Crestline with Fort Wayne, Ind. A line from Fort Wayne to Chicago—the Fort Wayne & Chicago—was chartered in 1852. A series of stock transactions gave the PRR a portion of ownership in the O&I and O&P.

By 1856 the Fort Wayne road had completed only 19 miles of track and was out of cash, while construction on the O&P was barely creaking along. Things weren't much better on the O&I. Although the track was finished, the rest of the facilities necessary to operate the railroad were still on the drawing board. Awash in red ink, the fortunes of all three companies were looking rather dim even though the future needs of the region held great promise for railroads.

Eventually, the owners of the three lines consolidated assets to form a new company—the Pittsburgh, Fort Wayne & Chicago Rail Road. And, figuring prominently on its board of directors was none other than PRR's J. Edgar Thomson.

In 1858 the new company was able to raise enough capital to buy new locomotives and rolling stock and complete a bridge across the Allegheny at Pittsburgh to connect with the PRR. The news wasn't so good at the other end of the line, though. After Chicago-bound rails had reached Plymouth, Ind., work stopped again for lack of money. Thomson enlisted the aid of the PRR, which shipped secondhand rails and spikes—much of it from PRR's moribund New Portage Railroad in the Alleghenies—to the railhead at Plymouth, and activity resumed. The enthusiasm that went with the revival made the sale of bonds an easy way to raise badly needed cash, and construction continued at full speed.

On January 1, 1859, the tracks had been finished to Van Buren Street, near the present day Union Station in downtown Chicago. Still, there was plenty of work to complete before trains could be speeding along the entire PFtW&C in regular service.

Unfortunately, while construction was in the final stages on the Fort Wayne line, more money was being spent than could be covered by revenues from moving freight and passengers along those parts of the line that had been completed. Subsequently, the line fell into receivership. It was sold in 1861 to a new company called the Pittsburgh, Fort Wayne & Chicago *Railway*, which finished the year in the black. J. Edgar Thomson was on the board of the new company as well, but the PRR did not

Alliance, in eastern Ohio, was the crossroads for a cadre of PRR lines, the primary one being the Pittsburgh, Fort Wayne & Chicago main line. In this scene recorded around 1912, a westbound flyer finishes loading express at the Alliance station while an apparently vacant train stands at the ready to the right. Tucked in the station pocket track is a short connecting train. Note the men on the new signal gantry installing new semaphore signals. *Jay Williams Collection*

PRR locomotives assigned to the Western Lines were for a time lettered PENNSYLVANIA LINES as on this 2-8-0 posing with a train load of steel cylinders circa 1910. The location is the Jay Street yard in Fort Wayne, Ind. This appears to be a publicity photo staged for the S. F. Bowser Co. of Fort Wayne. *Jay Williams Collection*

have a controlling interest in the line.

The Civil War and the resulting increase in traffic was just the tonic the PFtW&C needed after its reorganization. Although the railroad was limited by its facilities as to the amount of freight it could handle, all profits were reinvested in the form of improvements in track and operating equipment, and slowly but surely traffic volume increased. By 1864 the railroad began paying its stockholders annual dividends of 10 percent.

Even before it was reorganized, the PFtW&C was attempting to advance its sphere of influence by making agreements with connecting railroads. (Use the map at the front of the book to navigate the complexities of these additions.) In 1860 the railroad leased the Cleveland & Pittsburgh, which ran from Rochester, Pa., on the PFtW&C main line, to Cleveland, Ohio, via Youngstown. Another lease that would serve the Fort Wayne well was that of the New Castle & Beaver Railroad which ran

from Homewood Junction, Pa. (also on the Fort Wayne road) north to New Castle, Pa., where it connected with the Erie & Pittsburgh, a line that eventually reached Erie, Pa. The Ashtabula, Youngstown & Pittsburgh brought the PRR north to Ashtabula Harbor, Ohio. The E&P was leased by the PRR in 1870; the AY&P, in 1873. Both provided access to docks on Lake Erie—lucrative gateways to PRR's growing coal and ore business—and both were feeder lines that characterized PRR's expansion tendencies during this period.

In 1865 the Cleveland, Zanesville & Cincinnati was purchased by the Fort Wayne. Known as the Akron Branch, it ran from Hudson, Ohio, south to Millersburg, crossing the Fort Wayne at Orrville. Later, the CZ&C was extended to Columbus.

Now that the PFtW&C was running in the black, its board was inspired to buy stock in lines that could feed traffic into the line. The Massillon & Cleveland was organized in 1868 to build from Massillon to Clinton, Ohio, through some of the richest coal fields in the area. Area mines were already producing 1,500 tons of coal a day, most of it heading to Cleveland via canal, so it was expected that the M&C would be an instant success.

The Panhandle

The year 1856 saw work on the Pittsburgh & Steubenville, a line that was to build southwest from Pittsburgh through the "panhandle" of Virginia (remember that West Virginia wasn't carved out of Virginia until the close of the Civil War) to meet the Steubenville & Indiana at Steubenville, Ohio, on the Ohio River. The grand scheme called for the P&S, the S&I, and other connecting lines beyond to provide a through route for the PRR to the Ohio River at Cincinnati, thereby siphoning traffic from the Ohio River—and probably from rival Baltimore & Ohio.

Toward this goal the PRR had bought stock in the S&I in 1854. The S&I was built but had to rely on local traffic until the P&S could be completed. In addition, the PRR had to build an extension from its terminal in downtown Pittsburgh to the eastern end of the P&S at what is now South Pittsburgh on the south side of the Monongahela River.

Unfortunately, construction of the P&S was foundering, and that—coupled to the lack of a bridge across the Ohio—in turn meant that the S&I was struggling to survive without the traffic it needed in and out of Pittsburgh. As a result, the S&I was forced into foreclosure in 1864.

Part of the problem was that Virginia was not too keen about letting the P&S cross its panhandle and the Ohio River and thereby compete for B&O's hold on east-west traffic. It took an act of Congress—literally—to get permission to build the bridge over the Ohio. The act also prompted Virginia to charter the Hollidays Cove Railroad to provide trackage east from the bridge across the panhandle some seven miles to the P&S at the Virginia-Pennsylvania border. After the Ohio bridge, the HC, and PRR's Steubenville Extension all opened in 1865, trains began operating through from Pittsburgh to Columbus, 193 miles.

Alas, the P&S and the HC were now both broke, and in January 1868 the Panhandle Railway Company was formed to run them. The PRR, which had over $5 million invested in the Pittsburgh-Columbus operation, had other ideas, though, and in May 1868 consolidated all concerned under the newly formed Pittsburgh, Cincinnati & St. Louis Railway. Despite the Panhandle's brief existence, "Panhandle" remained a

nickname for the line and some of its future extensions for at least the next century.

Thomson's visions did not stop at Columbus; Cincinnati, Indianapolis, and St. Louis remained on his mind. Independent lines were being finished that would link Columbus with all three of those cities. The Little Miami Railroad was headed from Columbus to Cincinnati, while the Columbus, Chicago & Indiana Central Railroad was reaching out to Chicago via Bradford, Ohio, and Logansport, Ind., as well as straight west to Indianapolis, where connections could be made to St. Louis via the Terre Haute & Indianapolis and the St. Louis, Alton & Terre Haute.

Pivotal Year: 1869

Before we can see how the PRR shaped events that took place in 1869 relative to its growth in the West, we have to take into account what was taking place in the offices of other railroads in the region. It appears that any proverbial flies on the wall would have had scorched ears (and wings).

Though times were good, tempers were heating up on the Pittsburgh, Fort Wayne & Chicago. The company saw PRR's formation of the PC&StL as hostile to the future of the Fort Wayne road, for it felt that the Panhandle's Chicago connection would be the death knell for any future through Pittsburgh-Chicago traffic currently on the Fort Wayne. Moreover, the directors were not happy that the PRR was the Fort Wayne road's only connection in the East.

Enter Jay Gould, a former New York

As of 1859, the PRR—or more precisely, the Pittsburgh, Fort Wayne & Chicago—had had connected all its namesake points. A little more than forty years after the fact, on July 22, 1899, we're witnessing the arrival of a PFtW&C special train behind 4-4-0 No. 48 at the suburban Chicago station of Englewood. In seven more miles the train will be at downtown Chicago. Rock Island tracks are in the foreground. *Railroad Museum of Pennsylvania*

CHAPTER 2

stockbroker who in 1868 had become president of the Erie Railroad. Regardless about what some historians might say about Gould's morals—or lack of them—he shrewdly recognized that a railroad which spanned half a continent was worth more than one which spanned only a state. With that in mind he set out to expand the Erie's holdings.

One of Gould's first steps was to lease the Atlantic & Great Western, which stretched from the Erie's west end at Salamanca, N.Y., southwest through Akron and Dayton almost to Cincinnati (intersecting the PFtW&C at Mansfield and CC&IC lines at Urbana and Dayton). Next he began talking with CC&IC management about leasing its Columbus-Chicago line, and then with the Rock Island about a lease that would get his trains from Chicago to Omaha—and consequently the Union Pacific.

Word of this reached PRR offices and fast action followed. Gould's terms for the CC&IC were outbid by the PRR with such speed that an inspection of the property was not done until after the paperwork had been signed. Through the PRR, the CC&IC was leased to the PC&StL in February 1869. Not to be outdone, Gould and his cohorts began buying stock and secured a controlling interest in the PFtW&C—the prize of course still being a route to Chicago (and therefore the Rock Island). With so much controlling interest, Gould could arrange the election of the entire board directors, set for March 1869, so that most of the parties nominated would be sympathetic to his cause. Although Fort Wayne directors didn't mind that Gould inflated the price of the railroad's stock, they *didn't* relish Erie's control of their railroad. In February 1869, the PFtW&C charter was amended such that the terms of only one quarter of the directors would be up for election at any time. Gould's attempt to stack the board would take two years, at least. Gould couldn't make money waiting around and so gave up on the effort.

The Fort Wayne's close scrape with Gould put the PRR lease deal that Fort Wayne directors had been negotiating in an altogether new light. They had been confident that a contract with the PRR would be all the protection the PFtW&C would need from the PRR. However, Gould had demonstrated otherwise, and the PRR leased the

PFtW&C July 1, 1869, thereby ensuring that the interests of both roads were protected by the larger railroad—which the PRR was fast becoming.

Grand Rapids & Indiana

One of the lines in which the PFtW&C had an interest involved a deal that also was closed in 1869. The Grand Rapids & Indiana Railroad had been chartered in Indiana and Michigan during 1854-55 to build a line from Fort Wayne to the Straits of Mackinaw via Grand Rapids, Mich. The northern end was to be built as a "land grant" road.

Land grant lines were popular in areas where the federal government owned all the land, the idea being to use land grants as enticements for railroads to build into territories that the U.S. wanted to settle. Once a railroad was complete, the government would transfer title to the land to the railroad, and in exchange the railroad moved government freight for free.

At the time, Michigan was a lumberman's dream, with more forest than open acreage. Forests meant on-line business (specifically, lumber), but once the land was cleared, it could be sold as farmland.

By 1856 Congress, through the State of Michigan, made a grant for lands between Grand Rapids and the shore of Lake Michigan at Traverse Bay, 190 miles. A combination of construction and financial problems besieged the GR&I, and by 1867 progress amounted to but a scant 20 miles of track laid north of Grand Rapids. The

The PRR reached Cleveland proper through acquisition of the Cleveland & Pittsburgh in 1860. The railroad ran a considerable number of passenger trains between Pittsburgh and Cleveland until well after World War II. The trains served this ornate depot on Cleveland's near east side rather than Union Terminal downtown, which was dominated by New York Central interests. *John Dziobko*

FACING PAGE: Two Alco freight diesels move an empty coal train along the Panhandle main— the old Pittsburgh & Steubenville—in the rolling Pennsylvania countryside west of Pittsburgh during the summer of 1963. *Richard J. Solomon*

The PRR reached Indianapolis in 1869 through its Pittsburgh, Cincinnati & St. Louis (later, the Pittsburgh, Cincinnati, Chicago & St. Louis) subsidiary. In this scene from the late nineteenth century, a PCC&StL passenger train stands ready to depart Indianapolis Union Station's east end. The ornate depot opened in 1888 and was still serving passenger trains at the end of the twentieth century. *Railroad Museum of Pennsylvania*

State gave the GR&I title for the lands adjacent to those tracks, but required completion of the second twenty miles of line by 1869. Once again construction stalled, placing the land grant at risk.

George W. Cass, then president of the PFtW&C, together with friend William Thaw came to the rescue, forming the Continental Improvement Company to finish the next 20 miles of track. Within a two-month deadline, the track was completed and $600,000 of construction debt paid off in exchange for $8 million of bonds and one million acres of grant land. Not bad for 60 day's work, but risky—building that much railroad in two months was no small feat.

With 1873 being the final deadline for the GR&I's completion, the Fort Wayne road agreed to finish the job in exchange for most of the line's stock. A contract was

drawn in September 1869 and assigned to the PRR. The road was finished to Petoskey in November 1873, and some 800,000 acres of land were transferred to the GR&I.

To St. Louis and to Cincinnati

With the west end of the Panhandle anchored in Columbus, J. Edgar Thomson continued to eye St. Louis. Thus, it was not surprising to see him join forces in 1868 with the Columbus, Chicago & Indiana Central, which in 1869 was leased to PRR's PC&StL following the J. Gould intervention mentioned earlier. The PRR now had its own route from Pittsburgh to Indianapolis as well as an Columbus-Chicago line.

West of Indianapolis, PRR's traffic was forwarded to the Terre Haute & Indianapolis and, west of Terre Haute, to the St. Louis, Alton & Terre Haute for the final leg of the trip to St. Louis, via Mattoon, Ill. Thomson's ambitions were for the PRR to own outright as much of the right-of-way as possible, so when the opportunity arose to build a new line more or less parallel to the StLA&TH, he jumped at the chance. The St. Louis, Vandalia & Terre Haute Railroad was born of the PRR-CC&IC partnership to link the TH&I with St. Louis. PRR built the line and took its pay in the new company's stock, and the TH&I promptly leased the new line, which was completed in 1870 as an almost arrow-straight route from Terre Haute to St. Louis via Effingham, Ill., and the one-time state capital of Vandalia.

Another gateway for the PRR was Cincinnati, which by the late 1860s boasted a population of over 175,000. As a river port and business center, the city supported both inbound and outbound railroad traf-

fic. The bulk of this freight came from B&O and Big Four Lines (New York Central) and was handled into Cincinnati via the Little Miami Railroad, which ran from Springfield, Ohio, south through Xenia (where it crossed PRR's CC&IC) to Cincinnati.

The LM, B&O, and Big Four were a strong force in Cincinnati and the PRR was viewed as a foe, so try as he might, Thomson had no luck wooing the Little Miami into the PRR fold. Undaunted, Thomson seized upon another opportunity to reach Cincinnati by having the PC&StL pur-chase, in 1869, most of the debt of the Cincinnati & Zanesville Railroad. This line ran west from Zanesville, Ohio, to Morrow where it connected with the LM to reach Cincinnati. The C&Z needed major work to bring it up to Panhandle standards; as well, 16 miles of new line had to be built from Trinway, Ohio, to Zanesville to link the C&Z with the Panhandle. Enhancing the C&Z's value, though, was the newly formed Newport & Cincinnati Bridge Com-pany, set to build a span across the Ohio into Cincinnati where connections could be made to the Louisville & Nashville.

Naturally, LM directors were upset at the PRR's advances. The LM had had a lock on commerce in and out of Cincinnati for years and had pocketed a bundle of cash in the process. When the B&O and Erie got their own lines into Cincinnati, though, LM directors panicked and con-cluded it was time to sit down with PRR interests. They negotiated a 99-year lease with the PC&StL which produced a better bottom line than the LM had seen hauling B&O and Big Four traffic. The lease went into effect in 1869.

Acquisitions in Hoosierland

The early 1870s saw the Panhandle lease the Jeffersonville, Madison & Indi-anapolis, which ran south from Indianapo-lis to Jeffersonville, Ind., an Ohio River town opposite Louisville, Ky. The railroad also had branches to Madison, Cambridge City, and New Albany, all in Indiana. Access to Louisville was by a bridge jointly owned with the L&N.

PRR President Thomson was still smit-ten by the expansion fever of the 1860s,

LEFT: Achieving St. Louis was a milestone victory for the PRR in 1870. For the duration of Pennsy's existence, St. Louis served as a turnstile for east-west traffic between PRR, Missouri Pacific, Wabash, Frisco, and Cotton Belt. In August 1966, PRR's *Penn Texas* noses into St. Louis at the close of its overnight trip from New York. The train once carried through cars to Texas via MP lines, hence its name. *Mike Schafer*

A big J-class 2-10-2 storms its way west through Bradford, Ohio, with a solid string of hoppers in the late fall of 1952. Bradford was on the Panhandle's old CC&IC Columbus-Chicago line. The line veering off to the right led back to the Columbus-Indianapolis main line at New Paris, Ohio. This cutoff plus the CC&IC between Columbus and Bradford gave PRR an ersatz bypass around busy Dayton. *R. D. Acton*

although now he was looking south. In 1865 and initially independent of PRR interests, the Indianapolis & Vincennes was chartered to build a line between those two Indiana points, the latter located on the banks of the Wabash River. Vincennes was seen as a portal to the South, the ultimate goal for the PRR being the Gulf of Mexico. The I&V opened to Vincennes in 1869. The PRR gained a controlling interest in the line, but its attempts to get all the way to the Gulf never materialized.

The "P Company"

All the new lines that had been amassed through lease or otherwise during the late 1860s and the 1870s stretched the capacity of PRR management to the breaking point. The leases of both the Fort Wayne and the Panhandle alone added up to better than 3,000 route-miles of track. There was new construction, purchases of locomotives and rolling stock, and maintenance of existing facilities to deal with—not to mention day-to-day operations.

Rather than move key people out of Philadelphia to manage the enlarged responsibilities in the West, the PRR decided to form a new company that could do so. This company would exist under the umbrella of Pennsylvania Railroad management but otherwise would be a separate operating entity. By 1871 the paperwork was done, and the Pennsylvania Company was born.

Essentially, the "P Company," as it was colloquially known, operated the PFtW&C and all its leased lines. However, the Panhandle Lines continued with its own management, operating all its owned and leased lines, as well as the CC&IC and the Little Miami railroads.

The plan had its flaws. All three of the semi-independent organizations converged at Pittsburgh, where all had their own facilities. Even with optimum coordination, Pittsburgh was an operational bottleneck that wound up placing the three companies at odds, and when things got backed up, operations sometimes ceased to func-

tion altogether. The PRR did not solve the dilemma for several decades until, in 1920, it regionalized the whole railroad, making Pittsburgh the Central Region which handled all its own operations.

To Toledo

Just about anything that would feed the PRR system was of interest to the railroad. A number of feeder lines were leased by the PRR even though they existed only on paper and the PRR had to actually construct them. One of the more important routes that fell under this scenario was that to Toledo, Ohio.

The Mansfield, Coldwater & Lake Michigan Railroad Company's line from Toledo Junction (near Mansfield on the PFtW&C) to Tiffin, Ohio, connected with the Toledo, Tiffin & Eastern Rail Road which ran north from Tiffin to Woodvale, Ohio. From Woodvale north to Toledo, the City of Toledo owned—and the PRR built—the Toledo & Woodvale Railroad. After numerous ups and downs, leases, and foreclosures, the three railroads and the resulting 79-mile route become the Northwestern Ohio Railway Company, leased by the PRR in 1879. The PRR now had a foothold in the Great Lake port city of Toledo.

A longtime goal of the PRR had been Cincinnati, which the railroad reached in 1869. On February 13, 1953, the *Union* awaits its departure from Cincinnati Union Terminal for Chicago behind a pair of EMD E7A locomotives, one clad in PRR's Brunswick green and the other in the celebrated Tuscan red. *Robert Malinoski*

LEFT: The PRR's entry into Toledo in 1879 would pave the way to Detroit a few decades hence. In 1963, a PRR transfer freight is about to swing onto the Maumee River bridge near downtown Toledo. *John S. Ingles*

THE PRR'S WESTERN EXPANSION

On a July morning in 1956, a GG1 electric calls at Wilmington (Del.) station with a Washington-bound express while a New York-bound train at far right drops off passengers. Wilmington sits within what was the last link in PRR's creation of a continuous New York-Washington route. The New York-Washington line was not built as a single endeavor. Rather, it was the result of combining several small railroads with PRR-sponsored construction projects, all of which was complicated by inter-railroad politics. Finally, in 1881, the Philadelphia, Wilmington & Baltimore Railroad closed the gap, creating the 226.6-mile line which today is a showcase, high-speed railroad. *John Dziobko*

The PRR's Eastern Expansion

MORE LINES IN PENNSYLVANIA AND TO THE ATLANTIC SEABOARD

Although the PRR was heavily focused on reaching Pittsburgh and expanding into the "West"—today's Middle West—during the second half of the nineteenth century, many significant expansions were also underway east of Pittsburgh. Through all this, PRR remained anchored in Philadelphia, but without lines to New York City, New Jersey, Baltimore, and Washington and elsewhere throughout the State of Pennsylvania, PRR's eminence in American transportation might have been severely stifled.

The Cumberland Valley Railroad

A number of connecting railroads at Harrisburg fed traffic to PRR's Main Line. One of earliest was the historic Cumberland Valley, chartered in 1831—15 years before the PRR. The CV ran west from Harrisburg across the Susquehanna River to Lemoyne, then southwest to Chambersburg, Pa., and on to Hagerstown, Md. As the named implied, the CV served the Cumberland Valley, an active hub of mining, manufacturing, and farming.

The CV made money for its stockholders after the original construction costs were paid off. The coming of the Philadelphia & Reading Railroad (of Monopoly fame, pronounced RED-ding) to Harrisburg siphoned off some of the traffic that the CV had been interchanging with the PRR, so in 1859 the PRR began buying stock in the CV to gain a controlling interest.

The Northern Central

The Northern Central was Baltimore's link to the Main Line of Public Works (Chapter 1). The Baltimore & Susquehanna Railroad, chartered in 1828, began building north from Baltimore, reaching York, Pa. in 1838. Naturally, the citizens of Philadelphia objected to this line, seeing it as a threat to the very commerce they were trying to bring east to Philadelphia over the Main Line of Public Works.

But the B&S pressed on, and in 1851 its main line reached the Susquehanna River at Lemoyne, opposite Harrisburg. Trains began running over the entire line that year, although they had been running on portions of it since 1831. Initially, horsecars had been used, then in 1832 a steam locomotive bought from George Stephenson in England revolutionized travel on the B&S. A branch from York northeast to Columbia fed that canal port on the Susquehanna and also connected there with the Philadelphia & Columbia.

Despite monies being scarce for expansion, the railroad aimed to extend itself another 54 miles up the Susquehanna to Sunbury to meet the Sunbury & Erie, which was building north to Williamsport, Pa., and on west to Lake Erie at Erie, Pa. Through alliance with the S&E, the B&S hoped it could siphon traffic off the Great Lakes that at the time was being routed to the Atlantic seaboard via the Erie Canal.

Another shrewd reason to build to Sun-

A trio of Alco FA/FB freight diesels—part of PRR's AF locomotive group—nose their way past PRR's Hagerstown, Md., depot with a hopper train on Aug. 4, 1956. Acquisition of the Cumberland Valley Railroad brought the PRR to Hagerstown and eventually beyond to Winchester, Va. This would be a useful route for the PRR because of the connection to the Norfolk & Western (a longtime PRR affiliate) at Hagerstown. *John Dziobko*

bury were the region's various coal fields. Those of the Lykens and Shamokin valleys south and east of Sunbury could be tapped by the B&S, while the mines of the Schuylkill (SKOO-kull) coal fields east of Harrisburg could be tapped by the Reading, which would feed to the B&S at Dauphin, Pa., a few miles north of Harrisburg. This whole arrangement would make coal shipments to Baltimore via the B&S more attractive than via PRR's more circuitous route through Philadelphia.

Partial financing was secured for the Sunbury extension, but construction stalled when the money ran out—in no small part due to the slim profits produced by the southern portion of the B&S. The B&S went into reorganization, the result of which was the 1854 emergence of the Northern Central Railroad. Work on the Sunbury line resumed immediately, and the whole line opened to Sunbury in 1858.

As time went on, it became apparent that the NC was hemorrhaging red ink. Although the railroad was handling anthracite coal to Baltimore and capturing at least a modicum of east-west traffic off PRR's Main Line route, the NC was a north-south railroad in a region of east-west trade. Considering the age of the road

south of York and the equipment that was running on it, it was surprising that trains were being run at all. After the election of Abraham Lincoln as President in 1860, the stock market plunged, and in that same month the State of Maryland attempted to foreclose its mortgage on the NC.

With things looking bleak for the Northern Central, it's no surprise that B&O president John Garrett and other speculators who had an interest in the NC sold their stock, probably at a loss. Much of it was purchased by none other than PRR President J. Edgar Thomson, later transferring it to the PRR. Not until 1900 did the PRR own a majority of NC stock.

Despite being the target of Confederate sympathizers—all of the line's bridges in Maryland were burned, and the road's offices at the Calvert Street Station in Baltimore were overrun by Maryland troops—the NC prospered during the war, thanks in part to Simon Cameron, President Lincoln's Secretary of War. Cameron had had a vested interest in the NC and routed much traffic over it to Washington and the battlefields. Too, the line carried considerable east-west traffic that had been forfeited by war-torn B&O. NC's improved earnings resulting from the war allowed its debt to Maryland to paid by 1862.

In 1863, the NC leased the Shamokin Valley & Pottsville, one of the lines that fed coal to the NC at Sunbury. The 27-mile road ran through the anthracite fields to Mount Carmel, Pa., and the lease included all the mines owned by the SV&P. Also in 1863, NC's influence was extended farther north through lease of the 72-mile Elmira & Williamsport, whose south end connected with the Philadelphia & Erie (formerly the Sunbury & Erie) over which the NC had trackage rights between Sunbury and Williamsport. The E&W's north end tapped the Erie, whose lines reached northwest to Buffalo and Rochester, N.Y.

The E&W lease was another one of those endeavors that looked better on paper than in real life. The E&W was in wicked shape, needing a massive dose of capital for equipment and trackwork. Further, the connection to the Erie included a car-to-car transfer of freight because Erie's six-foot "wide" gauge prevented an interchange of equipment. In 1872 after leasing the Chemung Railroad (Elmira-Watkins Glen, N.Y.) and the Elmira, Jefferson & Canandaigua (Watkins Glen-Canandaigua, N.Y.), the NC was able to interchange with the New York Central at Himrod Junction on the EJ&C, thus

LEFT: Invading the streets of York, Pa., in 1964, train 554 rambles along the old Northern Central en route from Harrisburg to Baltimore. A freshly painted Electro-Motive E7A locomotive leads the coach-only local, which provided a connection off the Chicago-New York *Pennsylvania Limited* at Harrisburg for Baltimore. *John Dziobko*

BELOW: Sunbury, Pa., became the northernmost point on the NC in 1858. It was also a junction point with branches to Wilkes-Barre and Mount Carmel. On August 17, 1956, the *Washington Express* makes its afternoon call at Sunbury. *John Dziobko*

The *Washington Express,* day train on the Buffalo-Washington route, pauses at Renovo, Pa., on the afternoon of Aug. 18, 1956. At this point, the train is on old Sunbury & Erie/Philadelphia & Erie trackage, which got the PRR to Erie early in the 1860s. The segment from Emporium to Buffalo was not added until late in the century. *John Dziobko*

bypassing the Erie until it finally figured out what gauge it *should* be.

NC's expansion also expanded its debt load, and eventually NC directors recommended to the stockholders that the line be leased permanently to the PRR. In 1875 the PRR integrated NC operations into its own. By that time, the PRR had purchased additional coal-field properties along the NC, bringing even more coal to tidewater and making the NC a more-attractive property. The NC continued to grow, and by the end of 1910 the PRR permanently leased the Northern Central.

The Philadelphia & Erie

Dating from the heyday of the canal boom of the 1830s, the Sunbury & Erie was a system of railroads projected to run from Sunbury to Erie. After securing financing, largely from Philadelphia interests and the State of Pennsylvania, the line was completed to Williamsport in 1855 and to Whetham (between Lock Haven and Renovo) in 1859. Later that year, rails were laid from Erie east to Warren, leaving a 150-mile gap from there to Whetham, though most of it was graded.

By 1861, the S&E still wasn't finished. During that same year, the State helped refinance the S&E's mortgage, at the same time renaming the road Philadelphia & Erie. Unfortunately, construction was further hampered by the Civil War, forcing P&E backers to consider a sale. The PRR was their immediate choice.

The heavily indebted P&E was leased by the PRR in 1862 and finally completed in 1864. Unfortunately, the hoped-for traffic never fully materialized despite improvements to the harbor at Erie. More money was injected, and the P&E sputtered along, its stiff grades west of Driftwood limiting train length; further, the traffic that originated via Erie's port never was very profitable due to stiff competition from the NYC.

The line had one asset that had not been exploited: easy grades east of Driftwood. As traffic on PRR's Main Line increased, proposals arose to create an alternate low-grade route between Harrisburg and Pittsburgh utilizing the NC to Sunbury, the P&E to Driftwood, and a new stretch of railroad from Driftwood west via Du Bois over the Alleghenies—the lowest crossing of same within the state—to the Allegheny Valley Railroad at Red Bank. From there, AV's route to Pittsburgh would complete the circuit. A PRR survey between Driftwood and Red Bank in 1868 confirmed that such a route would have lower ruling grades than the PRR Main Line.

The Allegheny Valley Railroad

Chartered as the Pittsburgh, Kittanning & Warren Railroad at about the same time as the Sunbury & Erie, this line was projected to run northeast from Pittsburgh over Allegheny Summit to Ridgeway and on to Buffalo. Construction started in 1854 at Pittsburgh, and the line opened as far as Kittanning by 1856. Edwin Drake's discovery of oil at the bottom of a 70-foot well at Titusville in 1859 caused much excitement in the valleys of northwestern Pennsylvania and changed the course of the AV. Goals for New York State points were set aside for a line to the new oil fields north of Kittanning which was completed to Venango City (Oil City) in 1868. The oil flowed, and the dollars did too, making the AV an important line.

The PRR had already tapped into the oil fields by this time, having jointly leased—with rival NYC no less—the Oil Creek Railroad in 1864. The OCRR ran south from Corry, Pa., on the Erie and the P&E, 27 miles to Titusville, a few miles above Oil City. Predictably, the joint arrangement went poorly, and in 1865 the PRR wound up buying NYC's share of the OCRR.

AV management never forgot their dreams of reaching New York state, though, and when they heard of the PRR's plan to build the "Low Grade Line" from Driftwood to Pittsburgh, the AV was quick to point out that it already had the charter to build such a route east from Kittanning. Both the AV and the PRR began collaboration and went to work. By 1874 the Red Bank-Driftwood line was open for traffic. Alas, the costs for construction came in at more than twice the estimate. The little AV was sunk despite record quantities of oil shipment. The line went into receivership in 1884 and was reorganized as the Allegheny Valley Railway; it was leased to the PRR in 1900.

To New York Harbor

Even as PRR President Thomson pushed his railroad west, it was becoming impossible to ignore the mushrooming ports of New York and northeast New Jersey. Although today it's difficult to imagine U.S. cities as being rivals to one another, other than in sports events, during the first century of this country, cities were indeed cutthroat competitors for trade and commerce, especially, New York, Philadelphia, and Baltimore. All of them served as ports of entry for import and export trade, particularly to and from England. All three cities were served by railroads and canals which moved goods between the ports and the West.

So cutthroat was the competition between ports that the State of Pennsylvania's annual report for 1858 cited a meeting of New York Central, New York & Erie, Baltimore & Ohio, and PRR officials whereby an arrangement was made to set general rates and eliminate unscrupulous salesmanship. Initially the authors stated the agreement was working, but eventually the PRR claimed that the NYC was not holding to the agreements. PRR retaliated by lowering freight rates for export/import traffic at the Port of Philadelphia, and B&O cut rates at Baltimore even more. But New York kept cutting the rates, too.

Pressured by Pittsburgh, Fort Wayne & Chicago and Panhandle interests for a direct line to New York, since most Western shippers desired to ship via that port, Thomson turned his attention to New York despite his loyalty to Philadelphia. Without its own route to New York, the PRR had to route time-sensitive New York-bound freight and passenger traffic from Harrisburg east via the Philadelphia & Reading

In 1967, Baldwin road-switcher 8050 prowls about old Camden & Amboy trackage at Camden, N.J. The C&A was one of several key railroads in PRR's quest to reach New York Harbor. Many of the railroads involved in that project later provided the PRR with access to burgeoning industrial areas. *F. R. Kern., Rail Data Collection*

One of the companies PRR acquired during its march to New York Harbor was the New Jersey Railroad between New Brunswick and Jersey City. In this interesting 1904 scene on the old NJRR at Elizabeth, a Jersey City-bound PRR passenger train behind a Class D16b 4-4-0 is about to cross above the Jersey Central main line. CNJ's Elizabeth depot can be seen at ground level in the distance, while the city's Socialist headquarters enjoys a nice view of both railroads. *Railroad Museum of Pennsylvania*

and Central of New Jersey. Unfortunately for PRR, the 180-mile trip over the P&R-CNJ was hardly long enough for the pair to discount their rates enough to help fight a war with NYC. Thomson's answer was to assemble a consortium of railroads and lines to extend the PRR's reach northeast to northern New Jersey and New York Harbor. Thomson commenced in 1862 by negotiating a traffic agreement with the Philadelphia & Trenton Railroad and the United Canal & Railroad Companies of New Jersey. With this established in 1863, the PRR set out to construct the Connecting Railway to bridge the six-mile gap between the PRR and the P&T. The line began at the PRR Main Line near what is today Zoo Junction northwest of center city and passed through North Philadelphia to a connection with the P&T at Frankford Junction. Trains used the P&T to Trenton, N.J., where they entered UC&RC lines to Jersey City.

Thomson started with the intention of leasing a single route to New York and wound up leasing a substantial system, for the UC&RR itself comprised a plethora of lines, notably: the Camden & Amboy (Camden-South Amboy, Bordentown-New Brunswick via Trenton); the New Jersey Railroad (New Brunswick-Jersey City); the Belvidere-Delaware Rail Road—"Bel Del" (Trenton-Manunka Chunk); the West Jersey Railroad (Camden-Millville via Glassboro, Glassboro-Bridgeton); the Cape May & Millville (Millville-Cape May); and the Delaware & Raritan Canal Company whose canals ran from Bordentown to New Brunswick and north along the Delaware River from Trenton to Bulls Island.

In addition to these and other lines, the PRR gained control of affiliated ferry services between Camden and Philadelphia, and between various New Jersey port cities and New York City. The mileage of all the rail lines operating within the system totaled 356; canal mileage was 66.

The PRR and the "United Companies," as the P&T/UC&RC group came to be called, wasted no time in getting into a

bickering match. Terminal facilities at New Jersey were inadequate, and though it was understood at the time of the agreement that new facilities were a must, the UC felt that they could ill afford to build them. Meanwhile, the PRR complained about high freight and interest rates on the P&T/UC&RC lease.

The costs of revamped or totally new terminal facilities were borne out of pocket by PRR although there was some compensation. For example, PRR received 22,500 shares of the UC&RR stock in exchange for the $3 million facility PRR built at Harsimus Cove terminal in Jersey City. PRR also constructed a coal terminal at South Amboy for the distribution, via water, of Pennsylvania anthracite and bituminous coal to the New York area.

PRR's annual report for 1874 cites "unrivaled terminal advantages at the cities of New York, Jersey City, and South Amboy." For the most part, the opposite was true. The facilities overall were in sad shape, save for the new Jersey City passenger terminal built that year—but at least on the Jersey side they were in the best location for future development, and now it could be said that the PRR served New York City.

To Washington, D.C., via the B&P

Since the 1861 lease of the Northern Central, the PRR had boasted a route from the West to Baltimore—heart of B&O territory. PRR and B&O then were rivals of the worst sort and as such the B&O subjected passengers and shippers transferring in Baltimore from NC to B&O trains to gross inconvenience and inflated pricing. For nine years the situation remained unchanged until the B&O advanced plans (again) to build a line to Pittsburgh. That got the folks in Philadelphia fired up!

Tit for tat, PRR's Annual Report for 1870 announced plans to build a line from Baltimore south to Washington, D.C., and then beyond to meet the Richmond, Fredericksburg & Potomac, which was building north from Richmond, Va. This was no easy trick, building a line almost entirely within the State of Maryland—the legislature of which was sympathetic to B&O interests. That fact was not lost on Thomson's men, and they had done their homework accordingly. Near the end of the Civil War in the mid-1860s, the PRR took notice of the Baltimore & Potomac Railroad, a line that had been chartered in 1853 by forward-think-

Backdropped by the lights of Manhattan across New York Harbor, a lone spectator witnesses the final train out of PRR's Exchange Place station at Jersey City on an evening in 1961. Exchange Place was a remnant of an era when the PRR did not yet have direct access to Manhattan. Passenger trains terminated at the Jersey City waterfront where Manhattan-bound passengers transferred to ferries. For 51 years after Pennsylvania Station opened in 1910 though, the PRR continued local service to Jersey City, along with the ferry transfer, for commuters destined for lower Manhattan. *Richard J. Solomon*

ing plantation owners to link Baltimore with the tobacco country on the lower Potomac River.

Investment money for the B&P had been slow to materialize, and surveys did not start until 1859. The B&O had been authorized to purchase B&P stock but elected not to. The charter plotted the main route from Baltimore to Popes Creek, Md., but a provision stipulated that branch lines could not exceed 20 miles.

In 1866 George W. Cass (recall the sweet gamble he made on the GR&I in the previous chapter) and his associates agreed to finance and construct the B&P. In February 1867 they received approval from Congress to build into the District, and later that year the PRR became involved. Some judicious mapping positioned a 20-mile branch out of Bowie, Md, to Washington.

Construction did not go without a hitch. Landowners along the right-of-way were charging top dollar for their land, and there was a proliferation of lawsuits and injunctions from angry supporters of the B&O. By 1873, though, the main line from Baltimore to Popes Creek was finished, and the line to Washington had been extended—through PRR subsidiary Alexandria & Washington—to Alexandria, Va., to meet

the Alexandria & Fredericksburg, which the PRR had opened in 1872 to close the gap between it and the RF&P.

As built, the B&P had no direct connection with the NC in Baltimore, so a half-mile tunnel had to be built to link the two lines. The PRR found it difficult to obtain the city's permission to build the tunnel, which was to be a terribly expensive endeavor to begin with, owing in part to B&O's clout in its home town. Construction started in 1871 and was not finished until 1873. The new line ran to the new Union Depot.

Of course, it wasn't long before the PRR began advertising direct service between Philadelphia and Washington. Without a direct Philadelphia-Baltimore link, though, trains had to run west from Philadelphia to York via Columbia, then south on the NC to Baltimore. Even with added mileage via York, travel time was the same as that over the more-direct Philadelphia, Wilmington & Baltimore-B&O route because of the one-mile horsecar trip between the two lines' stations in Baltimore.

The Last Link

The Northern Central had been in Baltimore since 1838, but as of the 1870s still didn't have access to decent terminal facilities on the harbor. The solution came in the form of the Canton Company, formed by a group of Baltimore businessmen. In 1870 they announced plans to develop three miles of waterfront property via a connecting railway to be called the Union Railroad. To ensure the project's success, they opened it to all Baltimore railroads. However, the B&O refused to cooperate, and the whole thing stalled.

The beginning of the B&P tunnel project in 1871 mentioned earlier saw the Union Railroad get a fresh infusion of cash, and work began in earnest to reach the waterfront. Completed in 1873, the line connected with the NC at Charles Street near the new Union Depot and ran northeast from there through a 3,400-foot tunnel to a connection with the PW&B at Bay View Junction and then down to the waterfront.

The PW&B had been in service between its namesake cities since 1838, however the link between it and the B&O and NC was—as a horse-drawn street-track operation—awkward at best. The new URR connection between the NC and PW&B made the PRR's case for a north-south routing over the PW&B road very attractive, and shortly after the URR opened, through PRR trains from Philadelphia and points north were rolling direct to Baltimore over the PW&B, shaving 55 minutes off the previously advertised time via York and making the run in eight hours.

The B&O's north-south business between New York and Washington, of course, took a beating, since the B&O still had to rely on a horse-drawn connection (later replaced by a ferry) to and from the PW&B at Baltimore. Although B&O freight and passenger traffic to and from New York Harbor had to move over PRR's New Jersey lines and was reaching its destinations with out impediment, the B&O in 1880 announced it would withdraw its freight and passenger business off the PRR's New Jersey lines.

B&O had lined up a new route for its traffic between Philadelphia and the Jersey City waterfront: Philadelphia-Bound Brook, N.J., over the Reading thence to the waterfront on the Central Railroad of New Jersey. At Communipaw, freight and passengers were transferred to ferry and car floats to reach Manhattan. The only snag

was a small section of the PRR that the B&O had to use in Philadelphia.

Early in 1881, red flags were raised by a newspaper article that revealed railroad speculator Col. Henry S. McComb's interest in reviving the dormant charter of the Delaware Western Railroad, which was to have been built parallel to the PW&B. After getting control of DW stock, McComb tried to sell it, offering it first to PRR, without success. Then he invited William H. Vanderbilt—of New York Central fame—to consider it and also went calling on B&O President Garrett. After the Delaware legislature voted to enlarge the DW's charter privileges, the PW&B reacted.

PW&B management approached Garrett, who quickly brought in Jay Gould, then on the board of Jersey Central. In mid-February 1881 Garrett's group agreed in principle to purchase 120,000 shares of PW&B stock at $70. The members of the syndicate then met with PRR vice-president Cassatt and offered him the opportunity of securing for the PRR a one-third interest in the PW&B. Cassatt declined the offer of such dubious bedfellows; McComb and Vanderbilt then declined as well.

In the end, and through some complex wheeling and dealing, PRR President George Roberts and Cassatt wound up buying a controlling interest in the PW&B on March 7, 1881. Garrett's failure to gain control of the PW&B was a bad break for the B&O. He had to rekindle negotiations with McComb, and it was announced on March 23, 1881, that the B&O had bought control of the Delaware Western. The line was constructed after the rate wars of 1881-82, giving B&O its own line from Baltimore to Philadelphia.

Garrett's new line opened in 1886, connecting at Philadelphia with ally Reading on the east bank of the Schuylkill. Now, through a cooperation with Reading and Jersey Central, the B&O had access to New York Harbor without any interference from the PRR—and none too soon. For two years already, the PW&B had been refusing to handle B&O trains or cars.

With the PW&B fully in its camp, the Pennsylvania Railroad had truly established an ideal New York-Washington route, destined to become a showcase railroad that would long outlast the PRR itself.🚂

Opened in downtown Philadelphia in 1930, Pennsy's Suburban Station exuded grandeur and class—no one expected less of the PRR in its hometown. This facility was just one of numerous projects undertaken by the Pennsylvania during the decades that followed the culmination of its territorial expansion in the late nineteenth century. Suburban Station was built almost adjacent to Broad Street Station (PRR's headquarters) in an effort to relieve congestion at "Old Broad," built in 1881 and closed in 1952. Suburban Station was the exclusive domain of PRR's electric-powered commuter trains that radiated in nearly all directions from Philadelphia. It still serves in its intended capacity. *Mike Schafer*

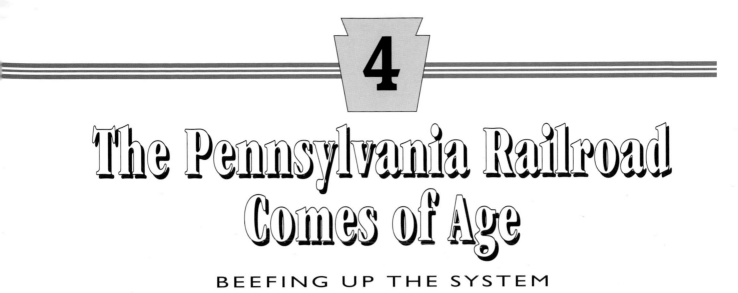

The Pennsylvania Railroad Comes of Age

BEEFING UP THE SYSTEM

As the 1880s unfolded, the PRR had, in terms width and breadth, pretty much culminated into the system that would be a familiar part of the U.S. railroad network for almost another century. The PRR system tapped into nearly every major city in the northeast quadrant of the U.S. Notable exceptions were few: Boston, Buffalo, and Detroit.

Overall, the 1870s had not been a particularly kind period for the PRR. A nationwide depression that began in 1873, ending the post-Civil War boom, brought a sudden decrease in business, severely curtailing PRR's healthy earnings and prompting the railroad to apply the brakes to its almost-relentless expansion. Then, in 1874, PRR President J. Edgar Thomson—arguably the most pivotal and influential leader the PRR would ever have—succumbed to heart problems. PRR Senior Vice-President Thomas A. Scott was elected to replace Thomson.

That depression spawned another unfortunate and this time embarrassing situation when the PRR cut wages systemwide: On July 19, 1877, train crews at Pittsburgh went on a strike that erupted into almost full-blown war. Local and state militia were called in to deal with a spectacular confrontation whose epicenter was the 28th Street roundhouse. Anarchy reigned for several days, most of it focused on PRR property throughout the city including Union Station and whole trains and locomotives, which were burned, looted, and otherwise destroyed, to the tune of $2.3 million.

The PRR sustained more losses a dozen years later in the famous Johnstown Flood. An unusually heavy, steady rain that began on May 30, 1889, disrupted rail service due to washouts and the subsequent loss of telegraph communications. On the afternoon of May 31, the dam on the Conemaugh River above Johnstown broke, releasing a 20-foot wall of water that wiped out virtually everything in its path for ten miles, including whole towns and most of the PRR; some 3,000 people perished. Locomotives and cars were carried downstream, as were some of the passengers aboard two sections of the *Day Express*, caught by the gush.

The damage closed the line to much of the traffic for nearly six weeks, with trains detouring by way of the low-grade route via Williamsport, Du Bois, and Red Bank. Losses were not limited to the Conemaugh Valley; east of the mountains, the Juniata also flooded, wiping out several miles of the PRR, the Philadelphia & Erie, and most of the remaining canals along the river. The calamity cost the PRR millions, not only in restoration work, but in lost revenues.

Certainly, the PRR did continue to expand up to and through the turn of the century, but many acquisitions were secondary properties that enhanced—but were not necessarily critical to—the overall system; very little was newly constructed

Train time at Manasquan, N.J., on the New York & Long Branch. The date is August 28, 1956, and a classic K-class Pacific—bumped from more prestigious assignments by diesels— heads up a long train comprised mostly of Pennsy's ubiquitous P70-class coaches. Built in the 1870s by Jersey Central as a means of getting New Yorkers to the North Jersey Coast for rest and relaxation, the NY&LB eventually became more of a suburban operation, feeding people to New York. CNJ and PRR became joint owners of the railroad in 1930. PRR's NY&LB trains changed from steam (later, diesel) to electric power at South Amboy, near the north end of the NY&LB, for the trip into Pennsylvania Station. *John Dziobko*

by PRR. Rather, most energies were focused on improving and unifying existing physical plant and operations.

PRR President Thomas Scott retired in 1880 and was replaced by George B. Roberts, who would lead the railroad nearly to the twentieth century. The railroad's most-significant addition during the Roberts regime was the acquisition of the Philadelphia, Wilmington & Baltimore. Because it was so integral to PRR's major Eastern expansions, the PW&B is covered in the previous chapter.

Notable Expansions after 1880

TO THE JERSEY SHORE: Opened in 1882, the 40-mile New York & Long Branch Railroad connected Perth Amboy, Long Branch, and Bay Head along the New Jersey shore. The NY&LB had been built by the Central of New Jersey in 1875 as an extension of its Elizabethport-Perth Amboy branch to tap tourist areas along the North Jersey Coast.

The PRR, of course, also had an interest in the booming resort area and in 1870 had already established through service between Philadelphia and Long Branch via the New Jersey Southern from Farmingdale; in 1875 it inaugurated service to Long Branch via the NY&LB from Sea Girt north. Then in 1881 the PRR extended its former-United Canal & Railroad Companies Camden-Whitings line to the NY&LB at Bay Head Junction. That wasn't enough, though. The PRR also wanted a piece of the New York-Jersey Shore action and threatened to build a line parallel to the NY&LB. CNJ acquiesced, signing an agreement with PRR on January 3, 1882, that allowed the PRR operating rights over the entire Long Branch. This would lead to joint ownership of the NY&LB in 1930.

Another resort area of New Jersey that appealed to PRR interests was that of Atlantic City on the Atlantic Ocean. Toward that goal, the PRR zeroed in on the Camden & Atlantic, which had opened between Camden, N.J., and Atlantic City (founded

CHAPTER 4

by the C&A) in 1854. The PRR acquired control of the C&A in 1883. (PRR tentacles were already attached to a number of other lines in the area—including a roundabout branch into Atlantic City from Newfield—partly through the UC&RC acquisitions covered in the previous chapter).

During this period, the PRR, through its control of the South Jersey clan of railroads (principally the West Jersey Railroad), built branches to other coastal points south of Atlantic City. Then in 1896, nearly all the lines, including the C&A, were consolidated into the West Jersey & Seashore Railroad. That railroad was leased to PRR in 1930, and in 1933 the PRR entered into an agreement with Reading Company to jointly operate the South Jersey network of PRR- and RDG-controlled lines as the Pennsylvania–Reading Seashore Lines to eliminate duplicate services and parallel tracks.

The integration of the South Jersey network into the rest of the PRR system resulted in the launching of through ser-

vice between New York and Atlantic City in 1890 and culminated with the opening of the Delaware River Railroad & Bridge Company span over the Delaware in 1896. This impressive bridge linked PRR's Philadelphia-New York main at Frankford Junction with the road's Camden-based lines and provided an all-rail route between Philadelphia and Atlantic City.

THE DELMARVA LINES: The growth the Delmarva (<u>Del</u>aware/<u>Mar</u>yland/<u>V</u>irgin<u>ia</u>) Peninsula as a farming region and source of seafood coupled with the growth of southeastern Virginia into a coal port and naval base led the push for a rail route down the peninsula to Cape Charles, Va., near the southern tip of the peninsula. From there, a 30-plus-mile ferry trip could put passengers and freight cars at any number of port cities in the Hampton Roads area. This approach to reaching Norfolk and environs was undoubtedly far less expensive than an all-rail route via Washington and would be less congested.

The vehicle for building the line was the New York, Philadelphia & Norfolk Railroad, which was the brainchild of PRR Vice President A. J. Cassatt. The NYP&N was an extension of a Wilmington-Delmar (Md.) line comprised of PRR interests (the Philadelphia, Wilmington & Baltimore and the Delaware Railroads). It was completed in 1884 but not folded into the PRR until the 1920s.

WESTERN LINES ADDITIONS: The Terre Haute & Indianapolis, mentioned frequently in Chapter 2, had long been a critical link to east-west PRR traffic between Pittsburgh and St. Louis but at the same time maintained its independence from the PRR. Finally, in 1893, PRR gained control of the TH&I and in the process acquired control of the Terre Haute & Peoria, a 166-mile line that ran northwest from Terre Haute to Illinois' second-largest city and secondary railroad hub (after Chicago, of course). An important connection at Peoria for the PRR was the Chicago, Rock Island & Pacific, which could channel Western traffic to and from the PRR, bypassing Chicago.

A related acquisition of the time was that of the storied Toledo, Peoria & Western, an east-west railroad that splices central Illinois (and greater Peoria) and which connected with the Panhandle's Logansport-Effner (Ind.) line on the east and the Santa Fe and Chicago, Burlington & Quincy on the west. PRR also considered this to be an effective Chicago bypass and acquired control of the "Tip-Up" in 1893, later splitting control with CB&Q.

Whereas the PRR finally had gained a route into Cincinnati in 1869 for traffic moving to and from the East, it was a circuitous connection at best for any traffic moving on PRR lines from Cincinnati to, say, St. Louis and Chicago. PRR addressed this problem with the 1888 opening of a route between Cincinnati and Richmond, Ind., the latter on PRR's Columbus-Indianapolis main line. This short (65 miles) but useful route was cobbled together by (1) the Pennsylvania Company creating the Cincinnati & Richmond Railroad—which actually built new railroad from Cincinnati to Hamilton, Ohio; (2) leasing Cincinnati, Hamilton & Dayton's line from Hamilton to the Indiana border; and (3) using a segment of the Richmond & Miami Railroad to complete the route into Richmond proper. Once at Richmond, traffic from Cincinnati could be routed over any of PRR's lines radiating from the city.

WESTERN NEW YORK & PENNSYLVANIA: PRR's largest acquisition during the final years of the nineteenth century added nearly 600 miles to the system and brought the PRR to Buffalo, N.Y. In 1900, the PRR acquired control of the physically and financially shambled Western New York & Pennsylvania Railway, which had a line from Emporium, Pa.—then on PRR's Philadelphia & Erie—to Buffalo via Olean, N.Y., as well as lines from Hinsdale (Olean) to Rochester, N.Y.; from Buffalo to Oil City via Corry, Pa.; and from Oil City to Olean by way of Kinzua, Pa.; and several branches. Purchase of the WNY&P gave PRR a cheap alternative to building a new line to Buffalo, and its addition to the system was a boon to PRR's heretofore struggling P&E line between Harrisburg and Emporium.

LONG ISLAND RAIL ROAD: Although a smaller purchase than the WNY&P, the Long Island Rail Road was in many ways just as critical to the PRR and certainly more high profile to the public. When chartered in 1834, the LIRR's purpose was to serve as part of an alternative transportation route between New York and Boston (utilizing ferries between the eastern end of Long Island and Stonington, Conn.). Instead, LIRR grew into a suburban railroad for burgeoning New York City. By the turn of the century, it had some 370 miles of line webbing the island, particularly the west end, all of which funneled into several terminals, notably in Long Island City (Queens) on the East River opposite Manhattan and in downtown Brooklyn.

PRR was particularly interested in the

fact that the LIRR was planning to tunnel under the East River into Manhattan. Realizing that this would be a boon to Long Island in general and the LIRR in particular, PRR gained control of the Long Island Rail Road in 1900.

PRR's own plans to invade Manhattan via a tunnel under the Hudson meshed perfectly with LIRR's similar project and undoubtedly would ease the obstacles facing both carriers in reaching this goal. For the LIRR especially, the PRR aspect made a good thing even better. LIRR's tunnel scheme was simply going to permit selected suburban runs to terminate at a location (or locations) in Manhattan where passengers could transfer to rapid-transit lines, and not at a major terminal. However, now allied with the PRR, the LIRR would be able to bask in the opulent transportation temple that was to be Pennsylvania Station, which with an ensuing electrification project deserves—and gets—its own chapter elsewhere in this book.

THE "SANDUSKY": Despite having a line to Cleveland and its port on Lake Erie, the PRR jumped at the opportunity to tap yet another port on that lake some 60 miles west of Cleveland, at Sandusky, Ohio. In 1902, in a move not unlike those of the late twentieth century when failed or superfluous railroads were carved up amongst the survivors, PRR bought at a fire sale the Columbus-Sandusky line of the bankrupt

Columbus, Sandusky & Hocking Railroad. The instant result was a new route to a port which the PRR could and would develop into an important rail-to-water transfer point for coal traffic off the Norfolk & Western at Columbus.

DETROIT: The Pennsylvania was a late arrival at the "Motor City," not gaining a direct entrance there until 1922, although it had reach nearby (54 miles south) Toledo in 1873. Even in the 1870s Detroit was twice as large as Toledo, but it wasn't until the 1910s and teens, when the automobile industry boomed, that the PRR seriously began to seriously reconsider the Detroit market, dominated by New York Central and its Michigan Central subsidiary. Backing PRR's Detroit desires was none other than Henry Ford himself, who with other Detroit interests pushed for an alternative to the MC/NYC alliance which had a stranglehold on the region.

The way by which PRR finally extended itself north from Toledo to Detroit was through the Pennsylvania-Detroit Railroad Company, created by the PRR in 1917. In reality, it was not an entirely new line per se but a consortium of interests willing to ally themselves with the PRR. From Toledo to the Michigan state line, PRR trains used the tracks of the Ann Arbor Railroad; from there, Pere Marquette tracks were used to Carleton, from which the P-D built a 20-mile cutoff line to River Rouge (site of a

With its NC8-class cabin car, an Electro-Motive switcher works the team tracks (public freight spurs) near Detroit's Fort Street Union Station the day after Christmas 1962. The Pennsy was a latecomer to "Mo-Town," long dominated by New York Central and Michigan Central. PRR's base of operations at Detroit was a small facility known as Lincoln Yard, located near a connection with the Wabash, a road in which the PRR owned considerable stock for a number of years. *Dave Ingles, collection of Mike Schafer*

Staying clear of downtown Pittsburgh, an A-B set of Electro-Motive F-units leads a freight eastward along the south side of the Monongahela River on a March morning in 1962. The train is negotiating a route put together in the late 1880s as part of an improvement project that allowed Panhandle freights to reach the Main Line route and Pitcairn Yard on Pittsburgh's far east side without passing through downtown. *Hank Goerke*

major Ford plant) and a connection to the Wabash Railroad. PRR passenger trains rode the Wabash into Detroit's Fort Street Union Depot. In return for PRR being able to use those various lines, the P-D revamped and enlarged Detroit-area freight terminal facilities for the use of Wabash, PM, and PRR. The first PRR passenger train entered Fort Street in 1920, but regular freight traffic did not begin until the River Rouge cutoff was in place in 1922.

Physical Plant Improvements

The late 1800s and early 1900s represented an era of unparalleled physical plant improvements for the PRR. Of course, the PRR had been making ongoing improvements from its very earliest days. As early as 1852, for example, traffic dictated the PRR to begin double-tracking between Harrisburg and Pittsburgh. But two tracks weren't enough, and in 1876 quad-tracking began, and by 1896 nearly the entire route between New York and Pittsburgh had been

transformed into a four-track "Broad Way of Commerce"—a term which would later inspire a train name.

The following paragraphs highlight PRR's more notable improvements some of which can be seen to this day:

TRENTON CUTOFF: The PRR seemed quite adept at making terminal and track improvements, particularly on its Eastern Lines. One of the earliest was the construction of the Trenton Cutoff. Opened in 1892, this 45-mile line linked the New York-Philadelphia main near Trenton with the Philadelphia-Harrisburg Main Line at Glen Loch, giving freight traffic between New York and the West a shortcut that bypassed the congestion of Philadelphia.

PITTSBURGH IMPROVEMENTS: Often an exasperating bottleneck for the PRR, the Pittsburgh region was ripe for several upgrade projects, one of the earliest being the development of bypasses for east-west freight traffic. Using the upgraded tracks and revised alignments of portions of PRR's Western Pennsylvania Railroad (the "West

Penn") together with a short stretch of new line, PRR in 1883 opened a bypass route around the north side of Pittsburgh for through freights moving between the Main Line and the PFtW&C. A similar bypass was created around the south side of town for through freight traffic moving between the Panhandle and the Main Line.

Part of the overall strategy for permanently detouring through freight operations away from downtown Pittsburgh was the construction of two new main yards. First up was Conway Yard, whose construction commenced in 1884 23 miles west of downtown along the north bank of the Ohio River on the PFtW&C main line. Four years later, construction began on the second facility, Walls (later renamed Pitcairn) Yard, some 14 miles east of downtown on the Main Line. To further facilitate freight traffic flow between the PFtW&C and Panhandle lines, the Ohio Connecting Railway (a PRR subsidiary, of course) built a bridge over the Ohio River a little more than a mile east of downtown Pittsburgh.

The main Pittsburgh passenger station was yet another scene of development. Following the Pittsburgh Riots of 1877 and the subsequent destruction of the second Pittsburgh Union Station, a third "temporary" structure was opened at the junction of the Panhandle and Fort Wayne main lines; this building stood until the 1901 unveiling of the present station building, which in 1997 still served, in a sense, as Pittsburgh's train station. More or less concurrent with the opening of the twelve-story building was the elevating of the station approach tracks to above street level.

A large train shed completed the station complex improvements in 1904.

ENOLA YARD AND THE LOW GRADE CUTOFF: Enola Yard began as a modest 12-track facility on the west bank of the Susquehanna River northwest of Harrisburg. In the early 1900s, the PRR embarked on a project to construct a heavy-duty freight route more or less parallel to the original Main Line between Harrisburg and the Trenton Cutoff and Philadelphia. The new route would have a maximum eastbound grade of 0.3 percent (versus 0.7 percent on the Main Line), and burgeoning freight traffic could be kept separate from the Main Line, thick with passenger trains.

This goal, which included the upgrading of the yard into a major classification facility to handle traffic out of Philadelphia and Washington as well as New York and New Jersey, was achieved through a combination of new track construction and the use of existing routes. Once the route was completed, New York-bound trains out of Enola Yard traveled southeasterly along an improved stretch of the old Northern Central to York Haven, Pa., where they entered new track which swung northeasterly to a connection with the Main Line at Parkesburg, crossing the Susquehanna River at Shocks Mill Bridge. East from Parkesburg, trains traveled on the original Main Line as far as Thorndale where they diverged on a new line that hooked up with the existing Trenton Cutoff near Glen Loch. The project was to include a low-grade freight-only line into Philadelphia proper as well, but it was never built.

PHILADELPHIA IMPROVEMENTS: The City of

Hard against the Susquehanna River, Enola Yard appears half empty (a good sign that traffic is fluid) in this 1946 view looking west from one of the humps. Track retarders are visible on each of the leads to track groups. *Railroad Museum of Pennsylvania*

tion—a ponderous, multi-story Victorian terminal initially used by nearly all PRR trains—intercity, local, and suburban—serving Philadelphia. The growth in traffic taxed Broad Street, and congestion problems were compounded by the fact that the depot was at the end of a short branch off the New York-Washington main line. This meant that through trains to and from New England, the South and the West had to make a backup move to reach the station.

In 1903 PRR opened a new, supplemental depot on the west bank of the Schuylkill River at West Philadelphia. This new station required a revised arrangement of approach tracks involving the Philadelphia, Baltimore & Washington (the Philadelphia, Wilmington & Baltimore until 1902) and the New York Division, as well as two new bridges over the Schuylkill. The two-level depot served New York-Washington trains so that they didn't have to make a back-up move into Broad Street. And since the West Philadelphia depot was positioned at the junction with the stub into Broad Street, trains to and from the Main Line route from Har-

ABOVE: Double-headed Altoona-built 4-4-0s are set to embark on a journey out of Broad Street Station, Philadelphia, circa 1890 with the *Pacific Express*. Not long after this photo was taken, the PRR began a massive reconstruction project involving the expansion of the whole Broad Street complex. The headhouse (partially visible behind the old wooden train sheds) was enlarged and a huge steel-arch train shed erected over the four original wooden ones, which were removed upon completion of the steel structure. *Railroad Museum of Pennsylvania*

Brotherly Love was the Pennsylvania Railroad's home town. The railroads headquarters were there for its entire history, and nearly all top officials lived in Philadelphia, mostly in the Main Line suburbs.

Hometown or not, early PRR operations in Philadelphia bordered on the chaotic, largely because of bewildering track arrangements. The downtown PRR rail hub from 1881 to 1952 was Broad Street Sta-

CHAPTER 4

risburg headed to or from Broad Street could also stop at West Philadelphia, allowing passengers to change there for destinations on the New York-Washington line.

While downtown passenger facilities were undergoing transformations, freight-related upgrades happened as well. One of the chief projects was the construction of the freight-only "High Line" trestle connecting the Main Line at 36th Street on the north fringes of downtown with the PB&W main and the Delaware Extension freight tracks leading to the waterfront. The High Line permitted traffic out of Enola—mainly coal trains en route to the Greenwich Point coal piers at South Philadelphia—to bypass Philadelphia freight yards.

In 1930, a modern Art Deco office building/depot dubbed Suburban Station opened adjacent to Broad Street, helping to ease "Old Broad's" congestion. In 1933, stately Thirtieth Street Station opened at 30th and Market, replacing the West Philadelphia station. Still a Philadelphia landmark and an important Amtrak station, Thirtieth Street served through trains on the New York-Washington line as well as suburban runs that originated at Broad and Suburban stations.

A new grade-separated connection at what became Zoo Junction was placed in operation in 1904, enabling passenger trains to pass more easily between the Main Line and the New York Division over the Connecting Railway. This led to the elimination of the Broad Street back-up move required by east-west passenger trains; those trains instead simply began making their Philadelphia passenger stop at North Philadelphia. Over the years, Zoo (it's adjacent to a zoological park) saw several improvements—mainly the implementation of "flyover" trackage—which provided uninterrupted passage of trains between the various lines radiating from Zoo.

WASHINGTON UNION STATION: Awkward terminal arrangements in the nation's capital for both the PRR and the B&O prompted Congress to pass bills in 1901 directing both companies to establish new, improved terminals and approaches. To carry out its own terminal project, B&O created the

Unfortunately, Broad Street's new train shed burned in 1923, leaving only the steel skeleton of the shed exposed. This view from the depot end shows the shed shortly after the fire and just prior to being razed. *Railroad Museum of Pennsylvania*

Chicago Union Station was (and is) that city's most-important railroad depot. The new facility, which rose on the site of the previous Union Station, was principally a PRR project, hence the station's family resemblance to New York's Pennsylvania Station. This westward view from September 1924 shows the concourse building under construction; the station headhouse and waiting room is the larger structure immediately behind it (the two buildings being separated by Canal Street). Track level can be seen below; the South Branch of the Chicago River is in the foreground. Pennsy tracks approached from both the north (Panhandle lines) and south (PFtW&C) sides of the depot, although all PRR passenger trains regardless of which division they came from normally approached from the south only. PRR successor Penn Central had the concourse building demolished in 1970 to sell the air rights for a bland office building that went up in its place, but the headhouse/ waiting room building remains intact and active. *Railroad Museum of Pennsylvania*

Washington Terminal Company. However, in what cynics might say was a rare act of foresight, Congressional leaders soon recognized the waste in having two separate nearby railroad terminals. B&O and PRR realized this, too, and in 1903 Congress repealed the two original bills, replacing them with new Act directing the two rivals to work together on a union station.

Pennsy's PB&W acquired a half interest in the WTC and all three companies went to work on the $16 million-plus project. WUS opened for business in 1907, a breathtaking granite monument to an unlikely cooperation between longtime foes. Union Station was stunning complement to the nation's capital as well, its architectural style mimicking those of other government buildings in the District, including that of the Capitol. It was and remains a true union station, serving several companies. In the Pennsy-B&O era, it also served Chesapeake & Ohio, Southern, and Richmond, Fredericksburg & Potomac.

NEW YORK HARBOR FREIGHT FACILITIES: For most of the twentieth century, Greenville, N.J., a mile and a half southwest of the Statue of Liberty, would serve as one of several important PRR freight facilities in the New York area. Land for same was purchased in 1889 to supplement Harsimus Cove a few miles to the north at Jersey City, but development was long in the making and did not begin until 1901. For one thing, the Greenville property lay some five miles east of the nearest PRR main

track. Under the guise of the New York Bay Railroad, a PRR subsidiary, lines were built east from the main line at Newark to Newark industrial areas and Greenville, finally reaching the latter in 1904.

"Mudville" would have been a more appropriate name for Greenville, for 22 million cubic yards of fill—much of it spoils from the tunnels under the Hudson River—were required to raise the property above water level and provide a firm base for a yard. But out of the mud rose a 1,200-car-capacity yard. Completed in 1907, the complex included extensive rail-to-water transfer facilities for PRR's fleet of barges, tugboats and lighters.

CHICAGO IMPROVEMENTS: The PRR was involved in another union station project in Chicago, where in 1881 the first Union Station for that city opened. The station was jointly owned by PRR's PFtW&C and Panhandle railroads and the Chicago & Alton, Chicago, Milwaukee & St. Paul, and Chicago, Burlington & Quincy railroads. Traffic quickly outgrew the facility, and in 1904 plans were initiated to replace it. The plans did not turn into reality until 1925, when the second Union Station opened. The new facility was operated under the name Chicago Union Station Company, with ownership of same shared by PRR, Burlington and Milwaukee Road, C&A having opted to become a tenant only.

Nearby to the new Union Station and predating it by seven years was the Pennsylvania Railroad's Polk Street Freight Station, a mammoth terminal that served downtown Chicago and the industrial area immediately to the west of the Loop.

World War I

Part of the delay in the construction of PRR's Chicago facilities and facilities elsewhere on the system as well as other improvement projects during the teens, had to do with World War I, which the U.S. entered on April 6, 1917. By the end of that year, the U.S. Government made the unprecedented move of taking control of most of the nation's railroads through the United States Railroad Administration (USRA). Even the now-powerful Pennsylvania Railroad was not exempt from this drastic measure.

The good news was that, the PRR undertook a number of improvements on infrastructure considered vital to the war effort. Thus, offsetting the wear and tear of wartime traffic were new bridges; increased track capacity such as on the PFtW&C, which was four-tracked between Canton and Alliance, Ohio; a major new yard and locomotive-servicing facility near Canton; and a general enlargement and improvement of other yards and engine terminals.

Nonetheless, the war did not leave the PRR in the best of shape, and the railroad had to spend considerable time, energy, and money during the Roarin' Twenties to rebuild itself. The centerpiece of this revitalization was a remarkable electrification project, covered in the next chapter. By the end of the 1920s, the PRR would be ready to face two more formidable challenges, the Great Depression and World War II.

The first half of the twentieth century also saw the PRR undergo numerous internal changes involving its bewildering array of subsidiaries, leases, and such—items far too complex and esoteric to document in a book of this scope. For example, many subsidiaries were consolidated into new subsidiaries. In 1905 the Vandalia Railroad was formed to consolidate all the lines that had been operated by the Terre Haute & Indianapolis and the Indianapolis & Vincennes. In turn, the Vandalia was consolidated into the newly formed Pittsburgh, Cincinnati, Chicago & St. Louis Railroad in 1916, which also absorbed several other PRR-affiliates, including the Pittsburgh, Cincinnati, Chicago & St. Louis Railway, which in 1890 had absorbed the old PC&StL covered in Chapter 2. Such corporate convolutions were ongoing throughout most of PRR's evolution after the turn of the century and could comprise a book of their own. 🚂

A few good things came out of World War I for the PRR, most of them involving upgraded infrastructure sanctioned by the federal government and its USRA. One of these projects was the construction of a new bridge over the Ohio River at Louisville. PRR's *South Wind*, en route from Florida to Chicago, has moments earlier departed Louisville and is shown trundling over the husky span into Jeffersonville, Ind., in 1966. *Collection of Mike Schafer*

Electricity moved both freight and passengers on the Pennsy. Two GG1 electrics rumble through the Harrisburg train shed with a freight as a Silverliner MU train steps out for Philadelphia in August 1965. Harrisburg was essentially the final extension of PRR's mainline electrification, in 1938. It was here that east-west through trains like the *Broadway Limited*, "*Spirit of St. Louis*," and *Liberty Limited* went through the ritual of exchanging steam or diesels for "motors," as electric locomotives are often called, for the trip to New York's Pennsylvania Station or Washington, D.C. *Ron Lundstrom*

5

The New York Extension and Electrification

PENNSYLVANIA STATION AND NEW ERA FOR PRR

One of the Pennsylvania Railroad's most-important improvement projects ever was its extension into Manhattan and the subsequent electrification of most of PRR's principal routes east of Harrisburg. Although in some respects the two projects were considered separate endeavors, in other ways they were inextricably interlinked. PRR's Pennsylvania Station project could not have been done without the technologies of railroad electrification, so it paved the way for an extensive electrification project that went well beyond Manhattan. For this reason, both will be covered in this special chapter.

Pennsylvania Station

Pennsylvania Station was one of the most ambitious railroad projects ever undertaken, dwarfing all other similar endeavors by its sheer magnitude. It was PRR's monument to itself and a gift to the people of New York. This grand station brought the PRR and new subsidiary Long Island Rail Road directly into Manhattan, thus ending arch-rival New York Central & Hudson River's access monopoly to the nation's largest city. The trans-Hudson crossing was the dream of PRR President Alexander Cassatt; the magnificent building, the work of architect Charles McKim.

Since 1871 the PRR had served New York City by way of its Exchange Place terminal on the west shore of the Hudson at Jersey City. Passengers to Manhattan were required to transfer from trains to ferries—a cumbersome proposition. Despite the lack of a direct route into Manhattan, the PRR handled an enormous volume of traffic to the growing metropolis. Although the railroad coveted direct access to New York, the Hudson River was a formidable barrier that could only be breached at great cost.

Alexander Cassatt found his railroad's New York access intolerable and hated the ferry crossing. He had investigated alternatives to ferries in the 1890s but lacked authority to bring about a solution. In 1899, when he became the PRR's president, he acted on his dream of direct train service to Manhattan. Most of the early schemes to bring the PRR into Manhattan involved bridges. The Hudson is nearly a mile wide, and one of the proposals involved a suspension bridge. This crossing alone would have cost an estimated $50 million—an enormous sum in 1900. At the time, tunnels were impractical since the operation of steam locomotives in a long tunnel would result in asphyxiation.

In 1901 Cassatt was visiting his famous artist sister, Mary, in France, when he had the opportunity to visit Paris' recently opened Gare du Quai d'Orsay, the first fully electrified railroad terminal in the world, with a long tunnel beside the Seine. Cassatt had found his inspiration: the PRR would tunnel beneath the Hudson and operate its trains electrically. On his return to the U.S., he put his plan into motion. To design the terminal he hired

ABOVE: Droopy-eyed DD1 electric No. 26 emerges from the Hudson River tunnels at Bergen, N.J., with a westbound train out of Pennsylvania Station circa 1911. Twin tunnels—actually concrete and steel tubes suspended in the riverbed silt—carried the tracks under the Hudson River from this point. *Cal's Classics*

McKim, Mead & White, one of the best known architectural firms in New York City. Both men had similar taste in culture. When McKim suggested a grand station building patterned after the Baths of Caracalla and the Basilica of Constantine in Rome, Cassatt was delighted. This was precisely what he had in mind: a great station in the image of classical architecture. It would feature tall marble columns and vast open spaces. To further this imperial image, Cassatt hired sculptor Adolph A. Weinman to adorn the station with giant stone eagles—ancient symbols of imperial power. Pennsylvania Station was not just a depot, it was a monument designed to inspire awe in generations of travelers.

Paving the way for a New York Terminal,

the PRR had purchased the Long Island Rail Road in 1900, planning at first to enter Manhattan in a long, somewhat backward route via Staten Island, Brooklyn and Long Island City. To this end, and to avoid interference from the New York Central, or anyone else who might disrupt its plans, the PRR secretly purchased property in Manhattan and New Jersey, as well as the LIRR itself, keeping both the western and eastern approach options to Manhattan open until work could begin. Preliminary work on the colossal project began in 1903, with plans finally stabilized for a trans-Manhattan tunnel route from New Jersey through to Long Island, and a bridge crossing of Hell Gate back to the mainland to connect with the New Haven Railroad.

Soon escavators were busily digging beneath the bodies of water which saddled Manhattan Island. Two sets of tunnels were needed, one under the East River for LIRR trains and PRR equipment being shunted to a new passenger-train servicing complex at Sunnyside, Queens, and one deep below the Hudson River to connect at Harrison, N.J., with PRR's main line to Philadelphia. Meanwhile Cassatt put his locomotive engineers to work designing a new generation of motive power (see Chap-

B1 electric 4751 switches a cut of head-end (baggage and express) cars at Sunnyside Yard, Queens, N.Y., early in the 1960s. Sunnyside was one of the largest passenger-train servicing facilities in North America and is still used today by Amtrak. Access to Sunnyside from Pennsylvania Station is via four tunnels under the East River that were also used by all Long Island Rail Road and New Haven trains arriving and departing Manhattan. *Allan H. Roberts*

ter 9). Relatively low voltage direct-current third-rail electrification was selected as the ideal method of powering trains in the new terminal. Construction of the station building began in June 1906.

Pennsylvania Station was ready for business by 1910. Service through the East River Tunnels was inaugurated first; LIRR trains began operating on Sept. 8, 1910. Service via the trans-Hudson tunnels took a little longer. The PRR wanted to make certain that everything was working absolutely perfectly and staged two weeks of fully orchestrated dry runs before actual service commenced; every train ran as scheduled—sans passengers—and every employee went through the motions of daily service as managers observed and worked out potential problems. Finally on November 27, 1910, the PRR began regular service into New York City.

When the station opened it was one of the most awe-inspiring structures in the Western Hemisphere. The *New York Times* described it as the ". . . [L]argest and handsomest in the world." Rows of gigantic Doric columns, made of pink granite from Milford, Mass., rose more than 60 feet high. A tremendous vaulted ceiling in the waiting room rose 150 feet above the floor, supported by eight huge Corinthian columns. Like many famous buildings of Antiquity, the main waiting room was fashioned from Travertine marble, imported from Italy. The waiting room's vast interior space, 110 feet wide and 300 feet long, was dwarfed only by the station's concourse and courtyard,

which combined were 340 feet long and 210 feet wide. This portion of the structure was built with granite and featured a complex structure of steel latticework columns and arches. The entire structure occupied two entire city blocks, more than 7 acres of land. Its tracks were located more than 40 feet below street level.

When Pennsylvania Station was fully operational it was the busiest through station in the world. Its 21 tracks, four East River tunnels, and two Hudson River tunnels handled roughly 1,000 rail moves daily. An automatic block signaling system installed in the Hudson Tunnels allowed for safe, bi-directional operation of up to 144 trains per hour.

Sadly, the two men most responsible for the station never had the opportunity to enjoy their greatest achievement. Cassatt had died of a weak heart at age 67 on December 28, 1906; McKim died Sept. 14, 1908, shortly after construction of the station building began. A large statue of Cassatt sculpted by Adolph A. Weinman greeted station passengers.

Pennsylvania Station served the railroad for more than fifty years. In a critical lapse of vision, a cash-starved PRR destroyed its grandest monument in the early 1960s to sell "air rights" over the station grounds. In its place an architectural monstrosity called "Madison Square Garden" was erected; all that remained of Pennsylvania Station were the tracks, platforms, and a glorified subterranean passenger concourse.

CHAPTER 5

PRR Mainline Electrification

One of the most intriguing aspects of the PRR was its extensive mainline electrification. Although a number of railroads experimented with electrification, the PRR's was by far the most comprehensive in North America, with nearly 800 route-miles—2,800 track miles—under wire. PRR's electrification was also among the most versatile in the U.S.: it was used by fast passenger trains, frequent commuter trains, and heavy freights.

In 1888 Frank Sprague made history by electrifying the Richmond, Va., streetcar system with an overhead direct current (d.c.) system. It was the first successful rail application of electric power, and it sparked a revolution. Within a decade, hundreds of electric street railways and heavier interurban lines were operating around the nation. Steam railroads were slower to adopt the use of electric power—the first steam-road electrification is credited to the Baltimore & Ohio in 1895 when it employed a short stretch of electrified track to avoid problems with heavy smoke in new tunnels around Baltimore. The PRR's first experiment with electrification followed later that same year.

In an effort to reduce operating costs on its lightly traveled Burlington & Mt. Holly branch in New Jersey, near Philadelphia, the PRR equipped the line with an overhead d.c. trolley wire. PRR's ridership had suffered as a result of new electric streetcar lines, and the railroad hoped to regain market share by fighting fire with fire. The scheme was viewed as an inexpensive experiment, but after 1900 the PRR would invest heavily in a far more substantial electrification scheme.

The advent of rail electrification is what ultimately allowed the PRR to build Pennsylvania Station. Furthermore, a disastrous fatal steam-train wreck which asphyxiated many people in NYC&HR's Park Avenue Tunnel in 1902 forced the issue. The wreck outraged the public and resulted in legislation banning steam locomotives in long tunnels in the city. If PRR's (or any other railroad's) trains were to enter the city, they had to be electrically powered.

To oversee the electrification of its project, the PRR hired George Gibbs, a talented engineer who had studied at the Stevens Institute in Hoboken and had worked for Thomas Edison. The railroad had to choose between two types of electrification, either low-voltage direct current or high-voltage alternating current, and the railroad tested both on its LIRR and WJ&S subsidiaries. A.c. required less copper and was more easily transmitted over long distances; however, a.c. motors and related equipment were much larger and more complex than d.c equipment.

There were several other considerations too. At the time, a.c. systems largely were untried, but d.c. electrification was relatively wide spread and had been in use for more than 15 years. So, the PRR concluded that low-voltage d.c. operation would be best suited for the Pennsylvania Station project, even if overhead a.c. electrification was later considered for more extensive plans. As it turned out, Pennsylvania Station was one of the last new installations of low-voltage third rail electrification on a major railroad in the U.S.

Soon the PRR was looking to explore other avenues of electrification. Its suburban Philadelphia commuter lines were suffering from extreme congestion at Broad Street Station, and in 1912 electrification was suggested as a way of reducing congestion and increasing capacity. The success of electric self-propelled multiple-unit cars (MUs) on the LIRR encouraged a similar operation in Philadelphia. The ability of electric MU trains to accelerate faster than steam-powered trains reduced running times and also eliminated the need for complicated terminal facilities. The PRR decided to electrify its Paoli and Chestnut Hill lines in 1913.

This new electrification had several radical features. It was PRR's first high-voltage a.c. overhead electrification and was very similar to that employed by the New Haven Railroad. With this system, the railroad diverged from early policy. On its previous electrification systems, it had built its own generating stations and produced its own electricity. With the Philadelphia electrification—and for all future PRR electrification endeavors—the railroad purchased electricity from an outside utility.

Another development implemented on this new electrification eventually affected the entire PRR system: the introduction of the position-light signal system. Instead of

PRR's Philadelphia-area suburban lines were the first to receive overhead a.c. electrification. Once all the suburban lines were "wired," the congestion at Broad Street Station was significantly reduced. MU trains such as this set of MP54-class cars at Manayunk on the Norristown branch eliminated the need to detach and turn steam locomotives from inbound trains; MUs could accelerate more rapidly and shorten schedules, and passengers liked the smoke-free environment of electric trains. *John Dziobko*

employing semaphore blades or colored lamps, a row of bright amber lights mimicked the position of an upper-quadrant semaphore signal aspects: a horizontal row indicates stop; a diagonal row indicates cautionary approach; and a vertical column indicates clear. Though unorthodox, this signaling system proved quite successful and was soon mandated for all PRR lines. The position-light signal has long since been an icon of the PRR.

The suburban electrification was very successful. The railroad's capacity was increased, schedules were tightened, and patronage increased. Passengers liked the new electric trains, which were clean, fast and comfortable. By 1928 the PRR had extended the wire on suburban routes to West Chester, Pa., and Wilmington, Del.

The PRR now viewed electrification as a potential panacea to other congestion problems. Its busy Philadelphia-Pittsburgh main line was saturated with traffic despite being four tracks wide in most places and having freight bypass routes. As early as 1908 the railroad had considered electrifying the line all the way to Pittsburgh, how-

ever by 1917 the PRR was only seriously looking at electrifying the Altoona-Conemaugh bottleneck. The steep grade over the Allegheny Summit was always a choke point, and certainly electrification could help relieve the pressure.

A prototype mountain electric, Class FF1, was built based on electric locomotives employed in mountain service on the Norfolk & Western. (The N&W had electrified a short section of its mountain main line in 1914 with great success.) However, a combination of events killed the Altoona electrification. The introduction of two new powerful types of steam locomotives—the I1s for freight service, and the K4s for passenger service—greatly improved mountain operations. The FF1 prototype had problems with its design, and would have required greater refinement before it was ready for mass production. But most importantly, the advent of World War I placed the PRR under the control of the United States Railroad Administration; the USRA was interested only in short-term solutions to PRR's traffic problems. It was not interested or willing to invest time, money, and resources in complicated electrification schemes.

Another route for electrification consideration was the heavily traveled line between New York and Washington. This was the busiest passenger line in the country, and through the 1920s its traffic was growing with no end in sight. The railroad wanted to maintain very fast service on the line, which it was able to do with its nimble E6 Atlantics and K4 Pacifics. Although existing electric locomotives could accelerate quickly, their safe speed topped out at about 80 mph, which was just not fast enough for high-speed passenger service.

Then in 1927, Westinghouse developed a revolutionary a.c. traction motor that was compact enough to fit between locomotive wheels, thus making a high-speed a.c electric locomotive possible. With this development, the PRR finally decided to electrify its line from New York to Philadelphia using the same a.c. overhead system it had employed on its Philadelphia suburban lines. In 1933, electrification was in place all the way from New York to Philadelphia. Soon the railroad extended its electrification plans all the way to Washington.

On February 10, 1935, electric train service was inaugurated to Washington D.C. The project was so successful that in 1937 the PRR began extending electrification toward Harrisburg. In the process it electrified several freight lines in Pennsylvania, New Jersey, and Maryland, including the Trenton Cutoff, the Columbia low-grade line, the Port Road line along the east bank of the Susquehanna River to Perryville, Md., and the line from Rahway to South Amboy and from South Amboy to Monmouth Junction, N.J. This enabled the PRR the flexibility it needed to haul most of its freight to New York, Philadelphia, Baltimore and Washington electrically, without clogging busy passenger routes. On January 15, 1938, the first electrically powered passenger train arrived in Harrisburg. Soon afterward, long electric freights were visiting PRR's vast Enola Yard.

This was the last major expansion of PRR electrification. Soon World War II and the introduction of diesel-electric power interrupted any plans for more electrification. In the early 1950s, the PRR did experiment with new types of electric locomotives (Chapter 9), and in the early 1960s it bought a new generation of freight electrics. The last advance the PRR made in electrification was during the mid 1960s, with experiments in high-speed passenger trains that led to the introduction of the *Metroliner*, high-speed MU trains designed and built by the Budd Company for 100-mph-plus intercity passenger service between New York and Washington. Ironically technical problems prevented the *Metroliner*s from entering regular service until 1969, the year after the PRR had merged with the New York Central. 🅿

On the morning of May 14, 1933, during the first weeks of the New York-Philadelphia electrification, a P5a motor drifts into Newark station with the *Red Arrow* from Detroit. The PRR was so pleased with the Philadelphia extension that plans were soon announced for electrification all the way to Washington, D.C., in 1935. As a side note, that same year Newark would get its own "Pennsylvania Station" when the railroad opened a distinguished Art Deco facility at downtown. That station today has been rehabilitated incorporating PRR signage despite the fact that the Pennsy has been gone for decades. *Cal's Classics*

Its sleeper-lounge observation lounge aglow following arrival from Chicago at Pennsylvania Station on the morning of March 16, 1966, the *Broadway Limited* awaits its shuffle over to Sunnyside Yard for cleaning and turning for that evening's trip back west. No other PRR passenger train was as well-known or highly regarded as the *Broadway Limited,* in its heyday one of the ultimate passenger trains in U.S. travel history. The train began running between Jersey City and Chicago in June 1902 as the *Pennsylvania Special*. The train was suspended from 1903 to 1905, and in 1910 its eastern terminus was shifted to the new Pennsylvania Station in Manhattan. The train was renamed *Broadway Limited* in 1912. The *Broadway* endured, remaining an all-Pullman train until 1967 and outlasting the Pennsy itself by 28 years until its 1995 indefinite suspension by Amtrak. *Robert Malinoski*

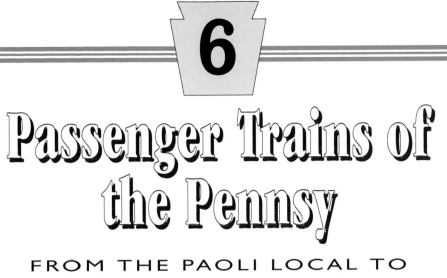

Passenger Trains of the Pennsy

FROM THE PAOLI LOCAL TO THE BROADWAY LIMITED

Railroads were built as much for moving passengers as for moving freight—and in many cases some lines were built largely for the transport of passengers. Because it had always served the most heavily populated region of the U.S., the Pennsylvania Railroad had a strong passenger traffic base for longer than most railroads. During railroading's pre-Depression golden era, the PRR moved 20 percent of the passengers who rode U.S. rails, and it did so with an almost incomprehensible network of intercity, local and commuter trains.

The Primordial Years

PRR bought its first passenger equipment—a baggage car and two coaches—in 1848 in preparation for the start of all-rail service between Philadelphia and points west of Harrisburg; additional equipment was purchased secondhand from other companies in 1850 and 1851.

A future component road of the PRR, the Camden & Amboy, is credited with offering both the first passenger cars to ride on "trucks" (rotating four- or six-wheel assemblies at each car end versus rigid car-mounted wheelsets) and the first coach to feature a center aisle with seats on either side. To another PRR affiliate goes the distinction of operating the world's first sleeping car. In 1836, the Cumberland Valley Railroad introduced a sleeping car named *Chambersburg* on its Harrisburg-Chambersburg (Pa.) night passenger train.

The first so-called "wide" passenger cars, which were nine feet wide, nearly the standard width of modern passenger cars, were introduced in Philadelphia-Pittsburgh service in 1858. By this time "smokers" and sleeping cars were also in use on the route, but the concept of en-route dining had yet to catch on. The first diners appeared on a future PRR affiliate—the Philadelphia, Wilmington & Baltimore—early in the 1860s.

PRR Passenger Trains Come of Age

Because of the outrageous speed offered by rail travel compared to other modes of the mid-nineteenth century, passengers were willing to put up with Spartan accommodations, much as they are now with flying. But as the century matured past middle age, railways flourished, and competition between railroads likewise escalated.

By 1870, passenger car construction had evolved from what were basically boxes on wheels into designs that had become widely accepted throughout America and which would last well into the twentieth century: longer cars with larger windows, full-length clerestory roofs for ventilation, air-brake systems, and coil-spring trucks.

Amenities such electric lights, "solid vestibules" (facilitating car-to-car passage), sleeping and dining accommodations were used to sway passengers who now had a

Immaculate D-class Atlantic 3155 leads the *Pennsylvania Special,* pausing for passengers at North Philadelphia in 1911. The following year this train became the *Broadway Limited,* the fastest, most prestigious train on the railroad. *Cal's Classics*

choice of rail companies to use. Improvements extended into the service arena as well. In 1870 the PRR entered into a contract with the new (1867) Pullman Company to provide and operate sleeping cars on overnight PRR trains—an arrangement that would last more than a century. In 1876, the PRR became the first railroad to introduce a "limited" passenger train; that is, a run that makes limited stops and/or features a limited number of cars so as to prevent crowding. The status was first applied to a Jersey City-Chicago train.

PRR passenger trains entered a new realm of distinction as the century waned and passenger trains everywhere entered their "plush" era. Most notable was the 1881 introduction of the *Pennsylvania Limited* between Jersey City and Chicago, at 26 hours and 40 minutes the fastest train on the route. PRR's newest and finest cars were always assigned to the *Pennsylvania Limited,* so the train went through several upgradings. In 1887, it became the first on the system to feature vestibuled cars. By the end of the century, the train had been described as a "work of high art." It now wore a custom paint scheme of green, cream, and red, and on-board services included a stenographer, barber, and maid. At that time, the *Pennsylvania Limited*'s

assigned seven-car consist included a combination baggage-buffet-smoking room-barber shop, a 40-seat dining car, four sleeping cars, and an observation-sleeper-lounge.

In 1885, PRR cornered the 225-mile New York-Philadelphia-Washington market, shared with rival consortium B&O-Jersey Central-Reading which operated the "Royal Blue Line" between Jersey City and Washington. PRR's *Congressional Limited Express* became the esteemed train of New York businessmen and Washington political leaders.

By the turn of the century, the New York-Chicago trade had become hotly competitive between the four principal railroads that served the market: New York Central System, Baltimore & Ohio, Erie, and PRR. Chicago had emerged as the nation's "Second City" in terms of size and importance, and travel and commerce between the two was immense.

Shortly following the turn of the century, PRR introduced another train to this key market. On June 15, 1902, the *Pennsylvania Special* set out to make passenger-train history, the four-car train making the 900-plus-mile run in 20 hours. In 1905 it was placed on an 18-hour schedule—faster than Chicago-Pittsburgh-New York passenger trains would make the run 90 years later. The train reportedly once exceeded 127 mph in Ohio. In 1912, the train's name was changed to *Broadway Limited* in reference to PRR's "Broad Way of Commerce" between New York and Chicago.

PRR's Passenger Fleet Post 1900

With the PRR immersed in the most populated quarter of the U.S., the railroad really didn't have to work hard to attract passengers. Pennsy was an institution, and people were well aware of its presence. Just about wherever PRR lines went, so did PRR passenger trains. PRR developed an astonishing network of passenger trains during the first half of the twentieth century and their operation was complex and laced with nuances. Because of this, the subject deserves its own book; but for purposes here, an overview will at least whet the appetite of passenger-train aficionados.

By sheer volume of trains and passengers, PRR's New York-Philadelphia-Washington route, which also hosted through trains to and from New England, the South, and the Midwest and a squadron of suburban-type trains, was (and is) an amazing corridor for passenger traffic.

Two early well-known trains that traversed PRR's main line to Washington were the *Federal* and the *Colonial*, both of which represented through *services* involving the New York, New Haven & Hartford Railroad between Boston and the Bronx and the PRR between Jersey City and Washington; a ferry carried passengers between the Bronx and Jersey City. Not until after Pennsylvania Station and the Hell Gate Bridge opened in 1910 and 1917 respectively was all-rail Boston-Washington service implemented.

Long PRR's signature train for New York-Washington service was the *Congressional Limited*, mentioned earlier. In 1952 it was upgraded with stainless-steel streamlined equipment built by the Budd Company of Philadelphia. Always popular with East Coast elite, *Congressional* service eventually was tripled by running a *Morning Congressional*, *Mid-Day Congressional*, and the *Afternoon Congressional*. Nonetheless, there remained plenty of other New York-Washington runs to choose from, trains like the *Embassy*, *The Speaker*, the *Constitution*, *Executive*, and *The President*.

In addition, the New Haven Railroad cooperated with PRR on a number of run-through Boston-Washington trains, including the *Senator*, *Patriot*, *William Penn*, and of course the *Colonial* and overnight *Federal*. PRR also relayed the trains of a number of Southeastern carriers north of Washington to New York, principally the Florida trains of Seaboard Air Line and Atlantic Coast Line, but also trains to and from Atlanta, New Orleans, and Cincinnati operating over the Southern Railway and the Chesapeake & Ohio. As a relay player, PRR held the trump card, albeit a relatively short one—its 227-mile New York-Washington route was imbedded in the most densely populated area of North America, a market brimming with the travel-prone.

Second to the New York-Washington corridor in terms of passenger density was PRR's Philadelphia-Harrisburg-Pittsburgh trunk—the heart of the Pennsylvania Railroad. PRR's star run serving those end points was the overnight *Pittsburgher*, an all-sleeping car train complemented with dining and bar cars. This was the only New York-Pittsburgh PRR train to be streamlined, in 1939. Other principal New York-Pittsburgh trains over the years included the *Duquesne**, *Juniata*, *Pittsburgh Night Express*, *New Yorker*, and *Iron City Express**. These trains were, of course, augmented by numerous through trains between New York/Washington and Chicago, St. Louis, Cleveland, Detroit, and Cincinnati.

On Pennsy's primary East-Midwest route,. PRR had to slice the lucrative New York-Chicago pie with opponents New York

*For a time, this train operated west of Pittsburgh

During the 1920s, travel on all-Pullman trains such as the *Broadway* was extraordinarily expensive and only for the elite.You can be sure that these passengers enjoying fine cuisine on the *Broadway*'s dining car in 1927 aren't heading for the Bowery. *Railroad Museum of Pennsylvania*

Central, B&O, Erie, and Nickel Plate-Lackawanna. New York-Chicago was the path of what was unquestionably Pennsy's best-known passenger train, the overnight, all-Pullman *Broadway Limited*, which at its peak made the 908-mile trip in just under 16 hours—an average speed of nearly a mile a minute including stops. A 1934 public timetable listed the *Broadway*'s amenities: "Barber, Bath, Valet, Ladies' Maid, Manicure, Train Secretary, Writing Desk and Stationery, Stock Quotations, Newspapers and Periodicals, Terminal Telephones, Baseball and Football Scores."

Though the *Broadway* epitomized luxury rail travel during the first half of the twentieth century, it really catered to an elite clientele whose numbers where limited. PRR accountants knew that most of the other trains on the route had better revenue showings. Indeed, shortly after the *Broadway* (and its chief rival, NYC's *20th Century Limited*) was streamlined in 1938, patronage aboard the train was so light that PRR officials mulled about discontinuing it altogether. World War II had a short-term

CHAPTER 6

Two extremes of PRR passenger service are represented at South Newark on a warm summer evening in the 1960s. At left, GG1 4890 hums effortlessly away from the Newark station stop with a hefty *Patriot* from Boston. A popular train for business people returning to Washington after a day in Manhattan, the *Patriot* fielded a full complement of coaches, dining car, lounge facilities, and parlor service with day roomettes and drawing rooms. At the other end of the spectrum are the strictly straight-back-seats MP54 MU cars of a Trenton-New York local skimming past in the opposite direction. *Mike Schafer*

positive effect on the *Broadway* and on passenger trains throughout the U.S., and ironically the train long outlived the PRR.

Couldn't get on the exclusive *Broadway* but desired a well-appointed train whose schedule was similar? Then the *General* was the train of choice, a coach and sleeping-car train introduced in the post Depression years. There was considerable demand for overnight New York-Chicago trains that departed their terminal cities at the dinner hour and arrived their final destination at breakfast, and in 1939 the new all-coach

streamliner *Trail Blazer* joined the *Broadway* and *General* in this time slot.

The list of other PRR Gotham-Chicago runs was impressive, though few held the esteem of the *Broadway* and *General*. In 1934, one also could choose the *Manhattan Limited*, the *Fort Dearborn*, *Progress Limited*, and *New Yorker*, *Admiral*, *Gotham Limited*, and of course the long-lived *Pennsylvania Limited* (it lasted until 1971). Service was bolstered by a cadre of Chicago-Pittsburgh trains, principally the *Golden Triangle* and the *Fort Pitt*. A few New

THE
MORNING CONGRESSIONAL
Washington • New York

THE
SENATOR
Washington • New York • Boston

THE
AFTERNOON CONGRESSIONAL
Washington • New York

ALL-NEW Through and Through!

PRR's re-equipping of its *Congressionals* in 1952 warranted this full-page ad in *National Geographic* which featured artist renderings of car interiors. "These brilliant new Pennsylvania trains," the ad copy extolled, "are the finest ever developed for daytime travel. Operating over the busiest tracks, the finest roadbed in the world—they serve the East's largest, most important cities." The Budd Company of Philadelphia built 64 stainless-steel cars for the *Congressionals* as well as for service on the PRR-New Haven *Senator.* As of 1997 some of the cars, now bearing Amtrak colors and markings, were still in regular daily passenger service. *Collection of Joe Welsh*

NEW COACHES are roomy. Deeply upholstered *reclining* seats — plenty of baggage space. *Separate smoking compartment with 14 lounge chairs.* Complete washroom facilities.

These brilliant new Pennsylvania trains are the finest ever developed for daytime travel. Operating over the busiest tracks, the finest roadbed in the world—they serve the East's largest, most important cities.

Accommodations for Coach and Parlor Car passengers are of rich quality for the mood of the moment . . . to work, relax or dine as you travel. In addition to facilities pictured, newest creations in handsomely furnished lounge cars are available for all.

Latest-type air-conditioning, colorful decor, fluorescent lighting, panoramic windows, electro-pneumatic doors, enclosed telephone rooms—and more —sum up to the most satisfactory trip you've ever taken by rail.

Enjoy the fine daily service provided by these great streamliners. It will be a pleasant NEW experience!

NEW PARLOR CARS with soft-cushioned *reclining* swivel chairs, deep-piled carpeting, attractive draperies, ample luggage space, wide package racks. Private drawing room with enclosed toilet annex.

NEW DRAWING ROOM PARLOR CAR on *The Congressionals.* Private rooms with divans, lounge chairs, wardrobes. Removable partitions permit use en suite. Enclosed toilet annexes.

NEW DINING CARS with all-electric kitchens designed for more efficient cooking. Wonderful service in a setting of charm comparable to fine hotel facilities.

NEW COFFEE SHOP CAR for Coach passengers. Complete meals or snacks prepared on electric radarange and electric grill. Served at counter or tables. Separate section with lounge facilities.

 PENNSYLVANIA RAILROAD

Go by Train . . . Safety—with Speed and Comfort

74

CHAPTER 6

York/Pittsburgh-Chicago trains such as the *Seaboard Express*, the *Metropolitan*, and the *Ohioan* operated west of Pittsburgh on the Panhandle via Columbus and Logansport.

PRR also offered direct Chicago-Washington service, though this was one market in which B&O played prominent with its highly regarded *Columbian* and the *Capitol Limited*, the latter still enjoying pre-eminent status under the Amtrak banner. PRR's best-known entry between this city pair was the *Liberty Limited*. In addition, most of the Chicago-New York trains made connections—either through or as a train change—at Harrisburg for Washington.

PRR's third major east-west corridor was that between the East Coast and St. Louis via Pittsburgh, Columbus, and Indianapolis with minor routing variations in Ohio. The "Fleet Leader"—to quote Pennsy timetables—of the 1,052-mile New York-St. Louis route was the *"Spirit of St. Louis,"* named for the biplane flown by Charles Lindbergh on his record-making trans-Atlantic flight. Supplementing the *"Spirit"*

with more basic services was the *St. Louisan*, and other principal New York-St. Louis runs, with Washington connections, included the *American*, the *Gotham Limited*, and another familiar name, the *Pennsylvania Limited*. Although the latter two were better known as New York-Chicago runs, both for a time fielded St. Louis legs out of Pittsburgh.

In 1941, Pennsy introduced the New York-St. Louis *Jeffersonian*, an all-coach streamliner catering to budget-conscious customers who still desired accommodations that were a cut above those found on other basic St. Louis services. In 1948, the New York/Washington-St. Louis market welcomed yet another new train, the *Penn Texas*, a streamliner that handled through cars to Texas, forwarded to Missouri Pacific trains at St. Louis.

In essence an offshoot of New York-St. Louis service, PRR also provided through East Coast-Cincinnati service via Columbus and the former Little Miami branch to the Queen City that out of Xenia, Ohio.

K4s 5490 is burning a nearly clean stack as it hammers along with train 204, the *Iron City Express,* at Foster, Ohio (between Cincinnati and Xenia) in July 1951. Clad in white attire, the 4-6-2's fireman acknowledges the photographer's presence. *R. D. Acton Sr.*

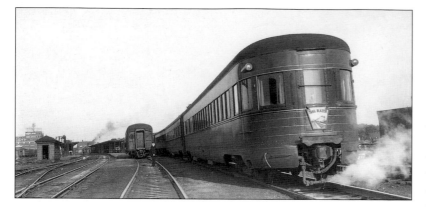

The all-coach *Trailblazer* catered to the budget-minded on the overnight New York-Chicago market. This morning view at Fort Wayne shows the westbound train's observation-lounge car, which was built by Altoona Shops in 1947. Though the photo information did not include a date, the pristine quality of the car suggest that the scene was recorded before 1950. *Cal's Classics*

The *Cincinnati Limited* was PRR's premiere train on the 755-mile Cincinnati-Pittsburgh-New York route; additional service was provided by connections and/or through-car service off of New York-St. Louis trains at Columbus.

PRR also tapped heavily into Cleveland—a city dominated by NYC. By way of connecting-train arrangements with its New York-Chicago and New York-St. Louis trains at Pittsburgh, PRR was able to provide service from New York and Washington to Cleveland on two different routes west of Pittsburgh, via Alliance and via Youngstown, Ohio. A 1939 PRR public timetable listed some eight daily trains in each direction in and out of Cleveland from the east, with the overnight New York/Washington-Cleveland *Clevelander* as the anchor train, supplemented by the New York-Akron *Akronite*. In later years, the *Steeler* name was applied to some trains

serving the Pittsburgh-Cleveland corridor.

Another strong NYC market invaded by PRR was Detroit, which Pennsy served from both the East and from Chicago. The long-established train serving the East Coast-Detroit market was the *Red Arrow*, supplemented by local and connecting services out of Pittsburgh.

The Chicago-Detroit market was nearly tied up by NYC, but PRR, working jointly with the Wabash Railroad (in which PRR owned considerable stock), provided competing service via Fort Wayne. Despite a respectable less-than-five-hour running time between Chicago and Detroit for the line's primary run, the *Detroit Arrow*—comparable to parallel NYC service—PRR bowed out of the market in the 1950s.

PRR had a three "intra Midwest" corridors: Chicago-Indianapolis-Louisville, Chicago-Cincinnati, and Chicago-Columbus. Though never a particularly strong market for PRR (nor its competition, the Monon), the Chicago-Louisville route nonetheless hosted passenger trains into the Amtrak era, which began in 1971, three years after PRR was merged out of existence. At one time the principal train was the *Kentuckian*, an all-Pullman overnight run. The *Louisville Daylight Express* and counterpart *Chicago Daylight Express* provided, as the name implies, daylight service. In addition, Louisville-Indianapolis schedules provided connections with New York-Pittsburgh-St. Louis trains. In 1940, the

The winds of war were already being felt when the *Jeffersonian* rolled into St. Louis on the afternoon of May 9, 1941. Leading the coach companion train to the all-Pullman *"Spirit of St. Louis,"* which would have arrived St. Louis only minutes earlier, was the 5338, one of four K4s Pacifics that received a semi-streamlined shrouding. *Cal's Classics*

CHAPTER 6

Chicago-Louisville route became host to a new Chicago-Miami streamliner, the *South Wind*, which PRR operated jointly with Louisville & Nashville, Atlantic Coast Line, and Florida East Coast.

Most Chicago-Cincinnati services operated via Logansport and Kokomo, Ind, but until shortly after World War II, the overnight *Southland*—initially a through train to Florida—operated via Fort Wayne. Day schedules were provided by the *Union* and, later, the *Red Bird*. By the 1960s, the *Southland* had been replaced by the *Buckeye*, a Chicago-Cincinnati/Columbus run combined with the *Kentuckian* between Chicago and Logansport.

Service to Columbus was handled by splitting Chicago-Cincinnati trains at Richmond, Ind., with the Columbus section heading east from there—and vice versa for westbound trains. The daytime Chicago-Columbus *Fort Hayes* was an exception, operating via Union City, Ind., between Logansport and Columbus.

The last principal PRR intercity passenger route covered here is that between Washington and Buffalo by way of York, Harrisburg, and Williamsport, Pa. Principal Washington-Buffalo trains included the *Buffalo Day Express*, counterpart *Washington/Philadelphia Express*, and the overnight *Dominion Express*. In the pre-World War II years the *International Express* provided a link to Canada; some trains on the route carried through sleepers to and from Toronto. The route included Williamsport-Harrisburg-Philadelphia runs, the most notable of which was the *Susquehannock*.

The Erie branch was served by trains out of Harrisburg as well as out of Pittsburgh via Oil City. The principal run was the overnight *Northern Express* and counterpart *Southern Express*, Erie-Harrisburg trains that carried through cars to and from Washington and Philadelphia.

Trains to Everywhere

The vastness of the PRR was such that, until after World War II, some sort of passenger service could be found on even obscure PRR branches. A random look at PRR timetables reveals the following sample of such services:

It's July 24, 1948, and K4s 5413 is slicing through the afternoon heat of the Ohio countryside at Dodson, Ohio, with train 207, the *Union*, bound from Cincinnati for Chicago. At Richmond, Ind., No. 207 will be joined with its Columbus section, train 907, and the combined train will reach Chicago by 9 p.m. PRR had the shortest route between Cincinnati and Chicago, but New York Central proved a worthwhile competitor thanks to a routing that tapped Indianapolis. *Tom Scholey*

A somewhat unremarked, obscure PRR passenger operation—but one fielding a full-size train with streamlined equipment—was that of the seasonal *Northern Arrow*. This was the featured train of the old Grand Rapids & Indiana, running from Cincinnati to Mackinaw City on the Straits of Mackinac, a popular tourist area. Two E8 locomotives have the all-Pullman *Arrow* in tow at Kalkaska, Mich., in summer 1961. *Hank Goerke*

In a scene that harkens to a time when trains were simply a way of life in just about every American town, a PRR motorcar makes an appearance at Freehold, N.J., during its daily wanderings between Trenton and Red Bank. "Doodlebugs," as such self-propelled were widely known, were ideal for lightly patronized branch lines. *John Dziobko*

●The *Nellie Bly* and other New York City-Atlantic City through services, which ended early in the 1960s.

●Williamsport-Canandaigua (N.Y.) service on PRR's Elmira (N.Y.) branch that handled through Pullmans between Washington, D.C., and Rochester, N.Y., in cooperation with NYC.

●Service between Wilkes-Barre and Sunbury, Pa., where connections were made with trains on the Harrisburg-Williamsport line.

●Service from Cincinnati and Fort Wayne to Grand Rapids, Mich., and the Michigan resort areas at Cadillac and Petoskey. The *Northern Arrow* was the distinguished train on this route.

●Eastern Shore service from Wilmington, Del., to Cape Charles, Va.: the *Del-Mar-Va Express* (day train) and the *Cavalier*, a night train which carried through sleeping cars to and from New York.

The Suburban Side of PRR

Several major U.S. railroads operated suburban train services in a number of major cities, among them New York Central, Burlington, and Southern Pacific. The PRR offered extensive suburban services in metropolitan New York and Philadelphia, and services of a more modest nature in Pittsburgh, Chicago, and Baltimore/Washington.

In Philadelphia, PRR built several stub branches to various outlying communities almost exclusively for suburban-train service: Chestnut Hill, Whitemarsh, Norristown, and Westchester. Nonetheless, PRR's most important commuter market here was that along the historic Main Line route west to Paoli. The "Paoli Locals" became an integral part of life in the posh suburbs strung along the Main Line—places like Villa Nova, Bryn Mawr, and Radnor. PRR also offered extensive suburban train service out of Philadelphia along the New York-Washington main line as far east as Trenton and as far west as Wilmington. Additional suburban service was operated out of Camden on the Pennsylvania-Reading Seashore Lines.

Kin to commuter trains were services of a local-type nature between Philadelphia and Harrisburg as well as between Philadelphia and New York City. Because of their on-the-hour departures from both New York and Philadelphia, the otherwise nameless New York-Philadelphia trains gained the nickname "Clockers."

In a sense, the Pennsy once fielded the most-extensive commuter-train network in north America—if you take into consideration the famous Long Island Rail Road, a PRR subsidiary from 1900 to 1966 which fostered the growth of countless bedroom communities all over Long Island. Similarly, PRR offered suburban train service out of Manhattan and Newark to numerous Jersey suburbs along the main line as far west as New Brunswick and well as to points on subsidiary New York & Long Branch.

Workers also rode to the nation's capital and to Baltimore aboard Pennsy suburban trains which plied the main line between Baltimore's Pennsylvania Station and Union Station in D.C. This modest operation included nearly a dozen commuter stops in the 40 miles separating Baltimore and Washington.

Another modest but diverse suburban-train network served Pittsburgh. Most PRR suburban service here concentrated on the 17 miles between downtown and Trafford east on the Pittsburgh Division Main Line. Likewise, PRR ran suburban trains on the PFtW&C main west to Beaver Falls, Pa. There were also some rather isolated suburban runs—in some cases only a single weekday train in each direction—serving Brownsville and Sharon, Pa., and Steubenville, Ohio, and as well as on the line to Buffalo. Alas, none of PRR's Pittsburgh suburban services survived past 1964.

PRR's suburban offerings in Chicagoland were meek at best, even in the pre-World War II years, with but two weekday trains in each direction between Valparaiso, Ind., and Chicago Union Station, about 44 miles. Surprisingly, the "Valpo Dummies," as they were known locally, outlasted the Pennsy by more than two decades.

As this book goes to press, the Pennsylvania Railroad will have been gone for some thirty years. Yet, intercity passenger trains still ply the Main Line between Philadelphia and Pittsburgh, and between New York and Washington, thousands of travelers every day whirl along former PRR tracks at 125 mph. Further, thousands of people daily board suburban trains at New York, Philadelphia, Baltimore, and Washington that are descendants of PRR commuter services. That one can witness all this even in an era heavily dominated by highways and airlines is testament to the Pennsylvania Railroad's influence on American transportation. 🚆

Despite the PRR's prominence in Chicago, its suburban services in the Second City were minimal—for many years only two trains a day between Union Station and Valparaiso, Ind. Here, one of the "Valpo Dummies," as the trains were known, arrives Chicago behind an Alco road-switcher in the late 1950s. *Al Schultz*

The PRR experimented with a few radical new passenger-train designs in the mid-1950s, the best-known probably being the General Motors *Aerotrain*. It test operated on the PRR as the *Pennsy Aerotrain*, running between New York and Pittsburgh (hauled by a GG1 between Philadelphia and New York, no less). On August 16, 1956, the lightweight speedster makes for an interesting contrast with the ancient buildings of Altoona as it heads for New York. *John Dziobko*

The PRR moved staggering quantities of freight traffic. Two freights are on the move—one eastbound, one westbound—on the old Pittsburgh, Fort Wayne & Chicago main line near Conway Yard west of Pittsburgh in 1966. *Ron Lundstrom*

7

From Coal and Steel to Produce and Merchandise

PENNSYLVANIA RAILROAD
MOVES THE FREIGHT

In April 1848, the Pennsylvania Railroad purchased its first freight rolling stock, 75 cars from carbuilder Kimball & Gordon. The following year, the road operated its first true freight train—that is, a train dedicated solely for the transport of freight on some semblance of an advertised schedule. The train operated twice a week over the Main Line between Harrisburg and wherever the west end of the still-abuilding railroad was at. Until that time, freight and passengers were often transported together, and we can speculate that schedules, if any, were haphazard.

Now fast forward 100 years or so. At the close of World War II, the PRR owned some 240,000 freight cars, and as the 1950s unfurled, the PRR was operating more than 2,000 daily freight trains. Although the PRR system constituted less than 5 percent of the nation's total railroad (route) mileage, which was close to 229,000 miles at the end of World War II, the PRR moved as much as 13 percent of the total freight carried by all Class I U.S. railroads.

With that kind of volume, it's no surprise that the PRR handled just about every kind of freight imaginable: perishables (fruit, produce, meat products); minerals (coal, iron, coke, stone, sand); petroleum and other chemical products; grain and grain products; lumber; livestock; machinery; and, of course, a vast assortment of manufactured goods—merchandise, if you will—from shoes to autos to refrigerators and furniture.

More than anything, prior to 1950, the PRR moved coal and iron ore. Most of the coal transported by the PRR originated at on-line coal fields scattered about Pennsylvania and moved to on-line industries (principally steel mills) or to Great Lakes and Atlantic ports and connecting railroads for forwarding to off-line destinations. In turn, iron ore—much of it originating off line in the upper Midwest and southern Ontario and shipped via the Great Lakes to PRR ports—flowed to the numerous steel mills served by the PRR.

There are basically three types of freight movement on most U.S. railroads: (1) local, that is, originating and destinating on line; (2) interline, which either originated on line and destinated off line or vice versa; and (3) "overhead" or bridge traffic, for which a railroad served only as an intermediate carrier. Prior to 1950, about a third of the PRR's freight traffic was local while the remaining two thirds were off line and interline.

From the time of their acceptance in America during the mid-1800s to the early twentieth century, railroads didn't have to do a great deal to attract freight business. Even at their worst, railways were still superior to horse-and-wagon or canal transport in terms of speed, economy, and efficiency. As cities and towns grew from infancy and rail lines flourished to form whole networks, transportation patterns began to emerge that dictated more specialized ways of handling both freight and

Mineral traffic—coal, ore, coke and the like—was a staple in PRR's freight diet. In this dramatic two-photo sequence, four PRR steam locomotives—two at the head end and two at the hind end—grapple with an ore train at Shamokin, Pa., headed for Mount Carmel, Pa. on August 17, 1956. By the time the helpers approach the crossing, a woman has paused at the parking barriers to absorb the action. *Both photos, John Dziobko*

passengers. Usually this meant separating them and running at least the passenger trains on schedules—with emphasis on overall speed for passengers. After all, freight itself wasn't wanton to complain about lengthy en route stops or delays.

The PRR was like many other railroads of the late 1880s and early 1900s when it came to moving freight. Large railroads were (and to a degree still are) organized into "divisions," a division's length generally being the distance a freight train moved during the course of a work day, usually between 100 and 150 miles, which then could take 10-15 hours. At each division point, where there was a main yard and engine terminal, locomotives and crews were changed.

Freight trains in those days were usually yard-to-yard operations. For example, a boxcar bound from Pittsburgh to Chicago might first move in a Pittsburgh-Alliance (Ohio) freight. At Alliance, the Chicago cars would await getting switched into an Alliance-Crestline train—a process that might take several hours, since all the freight cars off the train from Pittsburgh had to be sorted. Once the cars reached Crestline, they went through another sorting—and so forth until they finally reached Chicago, perhaps three, four, or more days after departing Pittsburgh. The only good news was that this was an extremely economical way to move freight, but shippers were at the mercy of the railroad as far as reliable delivery times were concerned.

That approach to moving freight began to change after World War I, with the coming of age of the trucking industry. In their embryonic form, trucking companies were basically harmless, but it didn't take long for them to start nibbling at rail traffic that was local in nature. During the 1920s, the emergence of a cohesive state and national highway system allowed trucking companies to compete with railroads over the long haul as well, particularly on time-sensitive freight.

This forced PRR and other railroads to tailor freight-train operation more to the needs of the customer. Although a great deal of the PRR's staggering array of freight continued to be handled in trains bearing a mixed consist—boxcars of merchandise, hoppers of coal, tank cars of chemicals, and such—much of it began being transported in trains dedicated to single types of commodities; i.e, merchandise-only freights scheduled for ideal delivery times at destination cities and "perishable" trains of refrigerator cars running on fast, strict schedules to minimize product spoilage. Freight operations in general became scheduled operations as customers demanded higher-quality service and greater reliability.

The result were trains that were "blocked" and scheduled, with cutoff times for acceptance of freight at a terminal or for cars arriving from a connecting train. Now, a carload of freight destined from Pittsburgh to Chicago might move in a train, say, blocked (grouped) with Fort Wayne and Chicago cars only. The train would still stop at division-point yards but only to change engines, cabooses ("cabins" on the PRR) and crews. Not until Fort Wayne would the train get switched, with Fort Wayne cars being pulled off and cars coming out of Fort Wayne for Chicago being added. Now the cars could get from Pittsburgh to Chicago within 24 hours.

PRR Yards

Railroad yards tend to be an evil necessity. They are a must for marshalling cars to and from connecting trains, and they are necessary for storing cars at ports and other terminals. Inevitably, though, yards always mean some amount of delay in the movement of freight.

Being in the thick of industrial America, the Pennsy was rife with yards of all types, from major classification facilities to simple holding or staging yards for nearby large industries to simple small-town terminal yards. Prior to infrastructure cutbacks and other rationalization which characterized U.S. railroads after World War II, the Pennsylvania boasted 152 yards. Fifty-two of these were considered "major," holding 1,000 or more cars. Three of those are of particular note—Enola, Altoona, and Conway, each of which had a capacity of 10,000 or more cars.

Although it might seem more logical for a railroad to locate its very largest yards at the largest cities it serves, in reality the most important yards on large railroads like the PRR tend to be at intermediate locations where traffic converges. Such was the case for Enola (Harrisburg) and Con-

Pennsylvania's Polk Street Freight Station dominated the sprawl of rail facilities that lay immediately south of Chicago's Loop. The fortress-like structure was completed during World War I and remained a landmark until it was razed in the 1970s. This artist's rendering provides a southwesterly view of the facility and the South Branch of the Chicago River. The rendering once hung in one of the building's main offices. *Collection of Mike Schafer*

way (Pittsburgh). All you need to do is look at the PRR system map at the front of this book to see why those two locations more than just about any other on the PRR were critical traffic funnels.

Enola was in essence the heartbeat of the whole PRR system. At its pinnacle, Enola comprised nearly 150 miles of trackage and routinely handled some 10,000 freight cars on a daily basis—double that during World War II. Facilities included "hump" (gravity powered) classification yards, repair shops, and an impressive engine terminal that catered to the needs of steam, electric, and diesel locomotives alike. In the mid-1950s, some 200 trains a day arrived and departed Enola.

Only 130 miles west of Enola on the Main Line lay Altoona Yard, with a 14,000-car capacity the largest on the PRR. Altoona Yard's purpose was considerably different than that of Enola and Conway. A portion of the yard space was used simply to hold freight cars that were scheduled for maintenance, repair, or rebuild at Altoona Shops or those that were built new at the facility and on their way out.

Another part of Altoona yard was used as a gathering point for traffic to and from numerous area branches, and yet another function of the yard was the reduction of train lengths for westbounds heading up and over the Allegheny Summit west of town; likewise, cars were added to east-bounds that had come down off the mountain. Relating to that process, helper locomotives were added to the hind ends of most westbound freights for the lift over the mountains.

Conway Yard, 23 miles west of downtown Pittsburgh on the line to Fort Wayne and Chicago, dates from 1884. It was built to facilitate traffic flow through and around greater Pittsburgh. In later years its importance as a hub yard for the PRR as a whole grew, and as a result, the PRR early in the 1950s embarked on a $34 million project to rebuild Conway. The yard was enlarged and modernized with hump-type classification systems, popular on many U.S. railroads after World War II. Strings of freight cars to be sorted are slowly pushed up over an artificial hill ("hump"); the cars are uncoupled and allowed to coast down into their appropriate track for sorting, with either remote-control or automatic retarders slowing them down along the way. Yard personnel use pushbuttons to align a car or group of cars into their assigned track.

Once completed in 1957, the "new" Conway allowed the PRR to restructure its freight traffic patterns and remove some of the burden from Enola Yard. At the same time, Conway cut as much as 24 hours out of east-west freight schedules and saved the PRR some $10 million per year in operating costs.

Other important freight gateways on the PRR are outlined herein.

NEW YORK CITY and environs, including Newark and Jersey City: Greenville Yard on Upper New York Bay was a gateway for traffic headed to and from New England via the New Haven Railroad. Much traffic through this yard was transferred to and from PRR's marine fleet of tugs and barges operating to Brooklyn and other Long Island points. A considerable amount of

CHAPTER 7

east-west traffic originated and terminated at Greenville. Just a few miles west at South Kearney, N.J., was Meadows Yard, an origination/destination point for traffic destined to Jersey points. In later years, Meadows saw much intermodal (piggyback and container) traffic.

MORRISVILLE YARD was on the far east end of the Trenton Cutoff (see Chapter 4) at Morrisville, Pa., just across the Delaware River from Trenton. This yard, revamped after World War II, primarily served nearby United States Steel. Classification was also done at Morrisville for traffic in and out of New York City and northern New Jersey.

PHILADELPHIA'S two major PRR yards were West Philadelphia and South Philadelphia. The former was a hump yard that processed mostly merchandise traffic and also freight (largely coal) off the anthracite branches. Busy South Philadelphia Yard, against the Delaware River, was the site of large coal and ore piers. Much mineral and grain traffic passed through this port-based yard, especially South American ore destined to steel mills at

Johnstown, Pittsburgh, and Bethlehem, Pa. A third facility of note in the Philadelphia area was Pavonia Yard in Camden, N.J. It was a joint facility of the PRR and Pennsylvania-Reading Seashore Lines.

WILMINGTON, DEL.: Edgemoor Yard was a pickup and setout location for through freights on the New York-Washington line. Much local traffic was handled out of Edgemoor to area industries, and scheduled freights for the Delmarva line and to Enola originated and terminated at Edgemoor.

BALTIMORE: Bay View Yard and Orangeville engine terminal comprised PRR's main freight facility in Maryland. Road freights off the old Northern Central originated and terminated at Bay View, which was located adjacent to PRR's New York-Washington main north of downtown Baltimore. PRR

INSET: Following Conway Yard's revamping in the 1950s, the PRR claimed it to be the largest pushbutton yard in America. BELOW: A westward view from about the middle of Conway prominently shows the engine terminal. At right are arrival and departure tracks, with freights in waiting. Barely discernible at far left is one of the yard's humps. Both views were taken in 1966 about a decade after the rebuild. *Both photos, Ron Lundstrom*

PRR's army of switch engines helped distribute freight along countless spurs and industrial lines. On a spring day in 1962, a Baldwin switcher with a string of boxcars and refrigerator cars in tow negotiates some of the maze of urban trackage that webs the Philadelphia area. *Collection of Mike Schafer*

had an additional facility, Canton Yard, at Baltimore Harbor serving the piers and a grain export facility.

WASHINGTON, D.C.: PRR freight traffic destined to the District per se usually went to Benning Yard in southeast Washington, but by far most road freights terminated and originated at Richmond, Fredericksburg & Potomac's huge Potomac ("Pot") Yard at Alexandria, Va., gateway to the Southeast.

HARRISBURG, PA.: In addition to Enola, already covered, Harrisburg proper had a yard. Located west of PRR's downtown passenger station, Harrisburg Yard was a staging point for local freight traffic and a setout/pickup point for Philadelphia-Pittsburgh freights that bypassed Enola. Coal trains and grain trains also changed crews here, and in later years Harrisburg Yard included intermodal facilites. Transfer freights linked Harrisburg Yard and Enola.

NORTHUMBERLAND, PA., near Sunbury, was a small town with a big PRR yard. Two large hump yards at Northumberland Yard classified cars for the Buffalo and Erie lines, so many road freight got worked over here. The yard also handled local traffic, such as freight off the Wilkes-Barre line.

PITTSBURGH: With such a heavy concentration of industries and a gaggle of PRR lines that congregated in the Steel City, PRR had to rely on several yards scattered about the area. Three are of note, including Conway, discussed earlier. Pitcairn Yard,

dating from 1888, was located on the Main Line on the east side of Pittsburgh. For many years PRR's princial Pittsburgh yard, Pitcairn's importance diminished once Conway was rebuilt in the 1950s. Scully Yard, due west of downtown Pittsburgh on the south side of the Ohio River, was originally the Panhandle's main Pittsburgh yard. Numerous transfer freights linked these and other PRR yards serving metro Pittsburgh and the steel mills.

CLEVELAND, OHIO: PRR had two facilities in this city dominated by New York Central. Kinsman Road Yard was the principal terminating/originating point for PRR road trains. This was a large facility, necessary for a city which abounded with industries. Whiskey Island Yard, on the Cleveland waterfront, featured an ore pier.

CINCINNATI, OHIO: Undercliff Yard was PRR's principal facility in the Queen City. Despite Cincinnati's size and its importance as a railroad gateway to the Southeast, Pennsy's facility here was rather small and inefficent.

LOUISVILLE, KY.: Pennsy's yard serving

Refrigerator cars laden with perishables dominate this hefty train drawn by two brutish E44 electrics, crossing the Susquehanna River on Shocks Mills bridge in 1965. *John Dziobko*

One of Pennsy's classic N5C "cabin" cars ("caboose" in PRR-speak) tags along at the end of a freight arriving at Buttonwood Yard in Wilkes-Barre, Pa., in the late 1960s as a Delaware & Hudson freight arrives from the north. The D&H provided an alternative gateway for New England-bound freight off the PRR. *J. J. Young Jr., collection of Gordon Smith*

this, another important gateway to the Southeast was not in Louisville at all but north of the Ohio River at Jeffersonville, Ind. PRR's main connection at Louisville was the Louisville & Nashville, and some PRR road freights operated directly to L&N's yard in Louisville via PRR's own impressive bridge over the Ohio.

FORT WAYNE, IND.: One of the more important yards on the old PFtW&C between Conway and Chicago was Piqua Yard on the west side of Fort Wayne. This large yard processed much agricultural traffic and was a hub for traffic from southern Ohio and Indiana as well as the old Grand Rapids & Indiana line.

LOGANSPORT, IND., though a modest-size city, was an active hub for the PRR in Indiana. Logansport Yard fielded traffic from seven lines converging on the city. Much Chicago-bound traffic was classified here rather than in Chicago.

TOLEDO, OHIO: Outer Yard was PRR's main freight yard in Toledo, and most road freights on the Detroit branch terminated here, not Detroit.

CHICAGO: The Pennsy was prominent in Chicago, and served the city through three principal yards and several smaller ones. The main facility was 55th Street Yard, used primarily by east-west traffic off the Fort Wayne line. Adjacent 59th Street Yard was used primarily by freights off the Panhandle and from Indianapolis and Louisville. Colehour Yard, located along Lake Michigan on the Fort Wayne main at Hammond, Ind., served as a gathering point for traffic off of both the Fort Wayne and Panhandle mains destined to the heavily industrialized area of South

Chicago, Ill., and Hammond-Whiting, Ind.

INDIANAPOLIS: Hawthorne Yard was PRR's main classification facility in the Indiana capital, serving the Pittsburgh-St. Louis and Chicago-Louisville routes as well as the Terre Haute branch. Hawthorne, on the southeast side of town, was supplemented by Junction Yard, PRR's interchange point with the Indianapolis Union Railroad.

ST. LOUIS: Rose Lake Yard near Washington Park, Ill., served St. Louis (Mo.) and the heavily industrialized area comprising East St. Louis, Madison, Granite City area east of the Mississippi River in Illinois.

Scheduling for Service

Early on, published schedules were a must for the movement of passengers. But as simple as that concept was, published (and adhered-to) schedules in the realm of freight transport did not become widely practiced until the early part of the twentieth century.

To overcome the inefficiencies of the more-traditional "yard-to-yard" movement of freight described earlier, the PRR after World War II began scheduling selected freights to bypass the "yarding" process. During the steam era, trains still had to stop at division-point yards to change crews and locomotives, however by not "yarding" a train, the railroad still saved hours of classification time. Eventually, the PRR—like a lot of U.S. roads—developed a whole network of "symbol" trains (PRR called them "Arranged Service" trains), so called because they were given alphanumeric symbols or codes which reflected their routes and/or services.

For example, train LCL-1 was a New York-Chicago run tailored for less-than-carload (LCL) shipments. It made the 900-mile trip in 32 hours while a sister train, LCL-3, ran from New York to St. Louis in under 37 hours. BF-14 was a Buffalo-Philadelphia run of general merchandise. Trains LD-1 (westbound) and counterpart LD-2 were the "Logansport Dispatch," running between that central Indiana Panhandle division point and Chicago.

Train CG-8 was a Chicago-Greenville reefer train that handled perishables such as meat from Chicago packing houses and fruit and produce from California. A similar run, MD-12, the "Manhattan Dispatch," forwarded fruit and produce from the Southeast to Greenville.

PRR even symboled and scheduled selected mineral trains—coal and ore trains that otherwise would have had to work their way slowly over the road on a crew- and motive-power-available basis. For example, PDS-3 was a solid coal train off the Norfolk & Western at Columbus, Ohio. PRR forwarded the train to the Elgin, Joliet & Eastern Railroad at Hartsdale, Ind., near Chicago, which moved the coal to nearby steel mills for unloading. Once emptied, the cars reversed their routing over the PRR to the N&W as train PDS-2. Tightening the schedule of such coal operations eased the crunch for hopper cars.

TrucTrain

Aided by government sponsored highway systems, the trucking industry became a formidable challenge to U.S. railroads in general after the Depression. Even today, it's hard to beat the economies of rail transportation, but in other arenas, especially speed, service and reliability, trucking began to excel markedly by mid-century. The PRR was particularly vulnerable to trucking because the Pennsy's network was comprised largely of freight routes of intermediate length: Washington-New York (approx. 225 miles), Pittsburgh-Chicago (about 460 miles); and Cincinnati-Chicago (less than 300 miles), to name a few. These are distances easily handled by trucks moving on Interstates.

The decline of mineral traffic after World War II, coupled to President Eisenhower's new Interstate Highway System, dealt a severe blow to PRR's freight revenues as well as those of most other railroads. For the first time in its history, the PRR was truly concerned about the future; it could no longer ride its laurels of being a rail transport empire.

Two of the PRR's most noteworthy postwar projects aimed at stemming the loss of freight revenues were its LCL service improvements and its full-scale entry into piggyback service. A drive to regain LCL service through more reliable scheduling, promotion, and additional merchandise representatives at major cities began in 1955. The downswing was reversed that same year, with the PRR handling 1.29 million tons of LCL versus 1.25 million tons the previous year. Ultimately, though, LCL became a lost cause; there was simply no feasible way for most railroads to compete with trucks in less-than-carload service. By the end of the 1960s—and the PRR—LCL service was negligible.

The news was much brighter on the piggyback front. The piggyback concept itself—whereby loaded truck trailers are transported on flatcars or trailers—was hardly a new concept in 1954 when the PRR launched its special piggyback service, dubbed TrucTrain. Piggyback had made an appearance as early as 1926, on the Chicago North Shore & Milwaukee Railroad, though it was a somewhat limited

The piggyback concept is readily illustrated in this scene of PRR TrucTrain trailers being loaded onto TrailerTrain flats at Kearney, N.J., in the mid-1960s. The PRR was the parent of TrailerTrain, later known as TTX Company, still a leader in providing nationwide car-pooling services. *TTX Company*

endeavor. PRR was one of the pioneers to embrace piggyback on a grand scale.

Pennsy's TrucTrain venture was really a combination of two operations. On one hand it was the railroad's own trucking service. The PRR would handle the entire shipment, picking up the merchandise with a truck, loading the truck trailer onto a TrucTrain, and unloading it at the other end to truck the trailer to its final destination. (Regulations restricted how far the railroad-owned trucks could distribute from terminals, usually only a few miles.)

On the other hand, PRR's TrucTrains also handled the trailers of common-carrier truck lines. Thus a truck belonging to a common-carrier company bound from Boston to, say, Kansas City could move via highway to Kearney where the trailer could be loaded onto a St. Louis-bound Truc-Train. The trailer would off load at St. Louis to be driven the remaining 280 miles to K.C.

Both types of trailer movements could be found on the same train, and Truc-Trains followed strict, express-style schedules, with little or no enroute switching. PRR's TrucTrains carried "TT" symbols. Trains TT-1 and TT-2 were Chicago-Kearney TrucTrains which made the run in about 26 hours—the fastest freights on the PRR. Success spawned more service, and soon TrucTrains were serving other city pairs such as Chicago-Baltimore, Pittsburgh-Detroit and Pittsburgh-Cleveland.

Specially equipped flat cars were necessary for the efficient handling of truck trailers, though regular flatcars were used in some early piggyback operations. To generate a pool of flat cars designed specifically for piggyback service, the PRR incorporated TrailerTrain Company, which began operations in March 1956. Other railroads were encouraged to purchase stock in the company and take advantage of the pool, and by 1964 forty railroads had done just that. In 1962, TrailerTrain began supplying flatcars modified for automobile transport, with bi- and tri-level "racks" for carrying 15-20 autos per car.

The firm survives today as TTX Company. It still provides railroads with a nationwide pool of standardized cars for trailer and container transport and is a legacy of PRR's final major triumph in rail freight transportation. 🚂

Three EMD diesels are in charge of train CB-1, the "Cannonball," skirting the banks of the Juniata River between Duncannon and Lewistown, June 10, 1965. This was one of PRR's real "hotshots," as described by the photographer. The train itself originated in Boston. The New Haven handled it to Maybrook, N.Y., where the Lehigh & Hudson River Railroad took over to take it to Phillipsburg, N.J. From here, the PRR handled it down the "Bel-Del" line to Morrisville and then west to Conway.
Robert Malinoski

The mention of Pennsylvania steam is nearly always synonymous with the road's K-class Pacifics (4-6-2s), specifically the K4s, one of which is shown making time with a NY&LB train in August 1956. Pennsy had 425 K4s/K4sa Pacifics, built by Altoona and Baldwin between 1914 and 1928. They hauled passenger trains, often double-headed on principal runs, on nearly every passenger route in PRR's sprawling empire, from the haute *Broadway Limited* to obscure secondary locals. For years the sight of two K4s' charging across Ohio or racing along the Juniata River in central Pennsylvania with the *Trail Blazer*, or any of PRR's other mighty limiteds in tow, was the very personification of the railroad. They spent their twilight years in secondary service before being phased out with most other steam power in the late 1950s. *John Dziobko*

The Steam World of PRR

PENNY'S RENOWN STEAM LOCOMOTIVE FLEET

The Pennsylvania Railroad locomotive fleet had humble beginnings, but as the railroad grew and prospered, its locomotive fleet grew accordingly. For most of the late steam era, the PRR maintained and operated the largest fleet of steam locomotives in the U.S. Furthermore, it operated more locomotives of some specific models than most railroads had in their entire fleets.

The Pennsylvania took an unorthodox approach toward steam locomotives. Its method of acquisition was unusual; it tended to design and build many of its own locomotives, and when it did purchase locomotives from a commercial builder, it usually provided all design specifications and rarely bought "catalog" designs. PRR's parts supply concept was revolutionary: early on it standardized its fleet, giving way to the company's famous slogan, "The Standard Railroad of America"—later revised to "The Standard Railroad of the World." Parts were interchangeable between locomotives of any given class, as were many parts between locomotives of different classes. Overall, PRR locomotives had a number of distinctive features. A favorite example were the fireboxes: while most lines used radial stay fireboxes, the PRR preferred the boxy Belpaire variety.

Generally speaking the railroad had a fairly conservative approach toward new motive power. It preferred tried-and-true models over radical designs and was not particularly interested in gadgetry. Designs stressed ease of maintenance over fuel economy, since coal—right in the PRR's back yard—was cheap and plentiful. Yet, the PRR did experiment with new models, and by doing so refined its power to new levels of excellence. Only after elaborate and methodical testing would the railroad conclude it had found a suitable design. Once it perfected the new model, it would mass produce it with little variation, often for decades. Its locomotives saw rough service, but were generally well maintained.

The Pennsylvania was strongly tied to the coal industry, and this led to the railroad's allegiance to steam power for much longer than other roads. The PRR's steam commitment ran through World War II, when most railroads were ordering diesels in vast quantities. The PRR continued to refine steam technology, even after the advantages of diesel-electric power had been accepted by most of the industry.

Early Years

In September 1849, the PRR received its first passenger locomotive, a diminutive Baldwin-built engine named *Mifflin*. It featured 14x20-inch cylinders, only a single pair of 72-inch driving wheels, and weighed 47,000 pounds. Earlier that same year Baldwin had also delivered the railroad's first freight locomotives, two 51,000-pound 0-8-0 types named *Dauphin* and *Perry*. With these locomotives, the PRR and Baldwin formed a working rela-

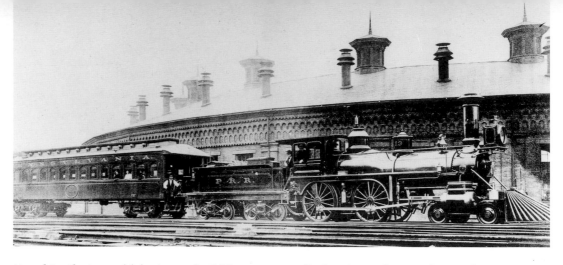

Class D1 4-4-0 No. 13 (formerly a Class A) poses with its crew and a coach. This was the first locomotive equipped with Westinghouse air brakes for regular service, in 1869. The photo was posed for the occasion. *Walter Lucas, Railroad Museum of Pennsylvania*

tionship that would last nearly 110 years. In the early years most of PRR's locomotives were built by Baldwin—then the foremost builder of locomotives in the U.S.—but the railroad was not shy to try other manufacturers as well.

In its first years, PRR named rather than numbered its locomotives. These names often reflected the nature of the locomotive. For example, two of its 66-inch driver 4-4-0 "American" types, designed to haul passenger trains, were named *Blazing Star* and *Gazelle*. In 1851, the PRR rostered just 21 locomotives, a fair amount for the time, but not enough for named locomotives to cause confusion. However the ranks soon swelled to the point where this colorful practice was no longer feasible. By 1857, with more than 200 locomotives the railroad converted to numerical identification.

The PRR investigated various locomotive developments over the years. In the 1850s and 1860s it looked to reduce the amount of maintenance on its locomotive fireboxes. Traditional iron fireboxes had a life span of only 6 to 12 months, leading the railroad to experiment with copper fireboxes, which lasted up to five years. Steel fireboxes replaced copper after 1862 when Bessemer-process steel became available.

Train braking on the PRR's mountain grades were a great concern from the very beginning of its operations. The inherent flaws of hand-operated brakes were exacerbated when descending the grade from Gallitzin to Altoona; the slightest error in judgment could result in a runaway. As a result, descending trains had to be kept relatively short.

A major breakthrough in train braking came in 1869 when George Westinghouse introduced the air brake. This system used compressed air to act on a pneumatic cylinder in each car. An air line running from a pump on the engine would allow the engineer to set the brakes throughout the train by applying air to the line. The cylinder would then press brake shoes against the wheels. (In 1872, this process would be reversed for fail-safe operation, with air pressure *releasing* the brakes.) Once again, the PRR was one the first railroads to take advantage of a new system that eventually became standard nationwide.

The John Bull

As explained in earlier chapters, the PRR absorbed many different lines during its growth. One of note was the Camden & Amboy, which owned and operated some historically significant locomotives. One in particular should be highlighted here.

In 1831, Robert L. Stevens ordered an 0-4-0 from the Stephenson Works in England. (Stevens was the son of early railroad visionary John Stevens mentioned in Chapter 1). Given the name *John Bull*, after the fictional character who personified the British working man, this 0-4-0 was among the first locomotives to operate in revenue service in the U.S.

Compared to later locomotives the seven-foot-long *John Bull* , with its 54-inch drive wheels, may seem tiny, but at the time it was considered a very large engine. A few years after its delivery, it was modified by the addition of a cab to protect the crew and a set of leading wheels to carry a "cow catcher," making it the first locomotive to feature this icon of American steam locomotives. Today the *John Bull* roosts at the Smithsonian in Washington, D.C.

Standardization

The Pennsylvania began building its own locomotives at its Altoona Works in

1866. In November 1867, Alexander Cassatt became the railroad's Superintendent of Motive Power & Machinery. He was instrumental in implementing a uniform system of locomotive class and design on the PRR that greatly improved the efficiency of its motive-power fleet—a system that had profound effect on the design of nearly all PRR locomotives for the next 80 years.

Originally, eight standard classes of locomotives were established. From 1868 to 1895 these were designated from A to G, with the A's being the most deluxe fast passenger engines and the G's the lowliest of switchers. Locomotives in each class were designed with interchangeable parts, and uniformity prevailed between classes as well. This system of standardization resulted in unprecedented operating efficiency not found on other lines of the time.

The eight original classes were gradually expanded to 25 classes. As the railroad's locomotive armada swelled to several thousand engines, the value of interchangeable parts was extremely advantageous. By 1910, the PRR had some 6,600 locomotives on its roster, by far the largest in the U.S.

PRR's Standard Fleet after 1895

CLASS D 4-4-0 (AMERICAN TYPE): In its early history, the PRR had more 4-4-0's on its roster than any other type of locomotive. It operated more than a dozen standard classes of 4-4-0, ranging from the lightweight Class D1 built between 1868 and 1872 with 68-inch drivers and weighing 77,700 pounds, to the relatively modern, heavy 4-4-0 Class D16d featuring 80-inch drivers and weighing 133,000 pounds. The D16b's were its most popular class of 4-4-0 of which the railroad built 262 between 1900 and 1908. After 1914, many were rebuilt with superheaters to Class D16sb.

Superheating involved recirculating hot steam through the fire tubes in the boiler, thus charging the steam with additional energy and increasing engine power.

The PRR continued to operate 4-4-0s until the early 1940s. Today D16sb No. 1223 is preserved at the Railroad Museum of Pennsylvania in Strasburg.

CLASS E 4-4-2 (ATLANTIC): The Atlantic type enjoyed great popularity on the PRR; the railroad operated nearly 600 of them in fast passenger service. The PRR first experimented with 4-4-2s in 1899. The most-well-remembered Atlantics on the PRR were the E6 class. From its first prototype E6 in 1910, which featured 80-inch drivers, weighed 208,700 pounds, and developed 27,409 pounds of tractive effort, the railroad honed the finest 4-4-2 to ever ride American rails. With the addition of superheating—creating the E6s class—the E6s were the epitome of fast passenger engines.

In 1914, the railroad built 80 E6s Atlantics at Juniata. These fine locomotives had 80-inch drivers, weighed 243,600 pounds, and delivered a phenomenal 31,275 pounds tractive effort—nearly as much as the K2 Pacific (4-6-2), but with 33 percent fewer driving wheels.

The research that produced the E6s eventually developed an even better passenger locomotive, Pennsy's famous K4s Pacific. Yet, the E6s remain as a shining example of PRR's steam prowess. Two of PRR's Atlantics are preserved at Strasburg, including famous E6s 460, which on June 11, 1927, raced a biplane . . . and won!

CLASS G 4-6-0 (TEN-WHEELER): Although the PRR began using Ten-Wheelers in 1852, the railroad was not as intrigued with this type as were other railroads. Yet, 4-6-0s were versatile and could be used in a variety of freight and passenger assignments. PRR's Class G3 and G4 Ten-Wheel-

Atlantic 5075 is the prototype Class E6 4-4-2, built by Altoona in 1910. In 1912, the year this photo was taken, the engine was superheated, making it a Class E6s, and its cylinders were enlarged from 22 inches to 23. *Cal's Classics*

Pennsy's G-class Ten-Wheelers were stocky little workhorses, perfect for local passenger trains such as this Pennsylvania-Reading Seashore Lines run photographed in south Jersey on August 21, 1955. The 5720 was one of 90 G5's mass-produced by Juniata Shops between 1923 and 1925; another 31 were built during that same period for subsidiary Long Island Rail Road. *John Dziobko*

ers were fast passenger engines used on crack limiteds until about the turn of the century when they were bumped to lesser assignments by the Atlantics. The G4a's were primarily for freight work. The early G-class locomotives did not feature PRR's trademark Belpaire firebox, which by the 1890s was being applied to most other types. For the most part the G3's and G4's were not common east of Harrisburg.

Interestingly, during the 1920s, after the Ten-Wheeler had been largely superseded by other more modern types of engines, the PRR took a renewed interest in the Ten-Wheeler and developed a whole new class of engines. In 1923, by using the same boiler found on its very successful E6 Atlantics, the PRR constructed a "super 4-6-0," Class G5s—the heaviest, and among the most powerful 4-6-0s ever built.

The G5s's were popular on short passenger runs, and spent most of their careers in commuter service. By 1953, most of the G5s' had been retired. PRR G5s No. 5741 is preserved at Strasburg, and LIRR G5s No. 35 resides on Long Island.

CLASS H 2-8-0 (CONSOLIDATION): The PRR was enamored with the "eight-coupled" Consolidation type, and it owned more of them than any other railroad (in excess of 5,000 units, albeit not all at the same time). The PRR first used the 2-8-0 wheel arrangement as early as 1864.

In 1876, the PRR established the type as its standard freight-hauler and took delivery of new 2-8-0s through 1916. In 1885, PRR introduced the Belpaire firebox—one of the everlasting trademarks of PRR steam—on its H1 Consolidations.

The Consolidation was not only PRR's

most popular type, it was also the most popular type ever built in the U.S., with an estimated 33,000 built over a 50-year period—thus giving PRR more than 10 percent of the total U.S. fleet. PRR found the 2-8-0's extremely versatile, using them in all types of service throughout its vast system.

The Pennsylvania had many classes of 2-8-0 which grew progressively larger and more powerful over the years. The H10s of 1913—considered the "standard" of PRR's Consolidation army—incorporated such modern features as a steam super heater (thus the "s"). The H10s featured 62-inch drivers, weighed 247,500 pounds, and with 205 pounds of steam produced 53,197 pounds of tractive effort—more than twice the power of some earlier PRR "Consolis."

While many of PRR's Consolidations were built at Altoona, others were contracted to Baldwin, Lima, and the American Locomotive Company (Alco). As mainline freight haulers, the Consolidations were frequently doubled and tripled to pull long, heavy drag freights. Standard practice after the turn of the century was to place four H6's on westbound freights leaving Altoona for the climb to Gallitzin; two would lead, and two would shove on the rear of the train, making for an impressive show of steam, smoke, and sound.

Today, two PRR Consolis are preserved, both at the Railroad Museum of Pennsylvania: Class H3 No. 1187, built by the Altoona in 1888 and Class H6sb No. 2846, a 1905 Baldwin product.

CLASS I 2-10-0 (DECAPODS): As its freight trains grew longer and heavier, the PRR searched for more powerful, efficient locomotives. Although the railroad could always add additional locomotives to heavy trains, every locomotive had the added expense of an additional crew. By 1916, the PRR was looking for a type of locomotive to replace its 2-8-0s—and even newer 2-8-2s—as its standard freight hauler. It found what it was looking for in the Decapod type—the 2-10-0.

The PRR built 598 nearly identical Class I1s 2-10-0's between 1916 and 1924. The PRR was very happy with the big "Dek's" performance, although operating crews were less than satisfied with the engine's ride quality. Known on the PRR as "Hippos," the I1's were so disliked by engineers on Lines West that they were rarely used

west of Pittsburgh. This was no hardship for the railroad, which found the I1s best suited in the mountainous Central Region.

The I1s were indeed big: they weighed 386,100 pounds, had 62-inch drivers, operated at 250 pounds boiler pressure, and produced an impressive 90,000 pounds of tractive effort—nearly 50 percent more than the older Class H6 Consolidations. The Hippos hauled several different tenders, but are probably best remembered with the gargantuan Class 210-F-82B tenders which carried more than 20,000 gallons of water and 30 tons of coal!

As a Class, the 600 I1s performed for nearly 40 years in the rolling hills of central and western Pennsylvania, as well as on the Elmira (N.Y.) branch—the heavy-duty coal route between Williamsport, Pa., and Lake Ontario. They were the last type of steam locomotive in service on the PRR.

One of PRR's Hippos escaped the merciless flames of the scrapper's torch. No. 4483 was stored for many years at Northumberland, Pa., along with other PRR preserved steam locomotives. Today it is in storage in western New York State.

CLASS J 2-10-4 (TEXAS TYPE): At the onset of World War II, the PRR found itself in a desperate motive-power quandary. Wartime demands had pushed traffic levels through the roof, but the railroad did not have adequate motive power to handle the surge. Furthermore, with the exception of the experimental S1 Duplex intended for high-speed passenger service, the PRR had not taken delivery of new steam power since the last M1a Mountain types were delivered in 1930. Complicating matters, wartime restrictions prohibited the PRR from developing new designs. The railroad had no choice but to swallow its pride, relinquish is world-renown self-sufficiency, and consider locomotives used by *other* railroads.

Ultimately it decided on the design encompassed by Chesapeake & Ohio's Class T-1 engines, the 2-10-4 Texas type. Although this design was more than ten years old, the C&O T-1 featured the qualities PRR desired, albeit without many of PRR's standard features. It was a super-powered locomotive featuring a trailing-truck with booster (that is, a powered trailing truck) and a large firebox with tremendous steam-producing capacity. As a result it performed well with heavy tonnage at high speed in level territory and at slow speed on stiff grades. It outperformed all locomotives then on PRR's roster. Undoubtedly, this type of locomotive is what the railroad needed, and between 1942 and 1944 PRR built 125 C&O-influenced 2-10-4's at its Altoona Works. When the PRR decided to do something, it did it

Burly I1 4644 stomps along Shamokin Creek near Paxinos, Pa., with a mineral train on a bright November morning in 1954. The "Hippos" were right at home lugging tonnage at modest speeds, hence they were common in the coal fields and in pusher service. Check out that tender—it's almost as large as the locomotive itself! Two more I1's were pushing at the hind end on, 119 cars back. *Robert Malinoski*

in a big way. Its J Class 2-10-4s were the largest fleet of Texas types in the U.S.

Sixty-five locomotives were Class J1, weighing 575,880 pounds. Another 60, Class J1a, were slightly heavier. They had 69-inch drivers and produced 95,100 pounds tractive effort.

The J's spent the war years hauling the railroad's tonnage west of Altoona. They performed well, but had short careers. By 1946, PRR was looking at diesels.

CLASS K 4-6-2 (PACIFIC): The Pennsylvania Railroad was initially very cautious about the 4-6-2. The type had been introduced in 1903, and only in 1907 did the railroad acquire its first experimental 4-6-2 from Alco. The railroad designated it Class K28 and studied it carefully before ordering any more. The PRR indeed had a need for a more powerful passenger locomotive. All-steel passenger equipment in part dictated by the new subterranean Pennsylvania Station in Manhattan was becoming the norm, and heavier trains needed locomotives stronger than the Class E6 Atlantics. To fill this need, PRR built 153 Class K2 Pacifics between 1910 and 1911. Another 72, slightly heavier, Pacifics—Class K2a—were built between 1911 and 1913, mostly by Juniata Shops and a few by Alco. These 80-inch-drivered Pacifics performed well and were soon hauling long all-steel passenger trains west from the end of the New York Terminal electrification at Manhattan Transfer near Harrison, N.J.

The PRR continued to experiment with the Pacific design, resulting in the 72-inch-drivered the K2b and K29 (1911); one of the two K2's was rebuilt with a superheater (making it a Class K2s) as was the single K29, making it a K29s. In 1913 the PRR ordered 30 new superheated Pacifics from Baldwin, Class K3.

In 1914, PRR introduced yet another new class of Pacific, the superheated K4s. This locomotive was a perfectly melded fusion of the experimental K29s and the excellent E6s. Prototype No. 1737 was delivered in May and proved to be a phenomenal success. This was not just a good class of Pacific; it was the best anyone at Altoona had ever seen. Weighing 302,000 pounds and featuring 80-inch drivers 27 x 28-inch cylinders, and a new variation of the Belpaire firebox, the K4s delivered 44,460 pounds of tractive effort. The K2's had only delivered 32,620 pounds.

After several years of careful testing, the PRR began mass-producing the K4s. Between 1917 and 1924, Juniata Shops and Baldwin built 324 of them. In a very short time, the K4s had become the Standard Railroad of World's standard passenger locomotive. The K4s became one of PRR's most famous mascots, and people the world 'round knew of the K4s' prowess.

When the PRR needed more passenger locomotives in the late 1920s, it built another 100 K4s, even though more powerful locomotives had been perfected. The railroad chose to double-head heavy trains with its reliable, prized K4s rather than risk a new design. When streamlining became the style in the late 1930s, the

PRR selected K4s 3768 to receive the Raymond Loewy treatment. This one-of-a-kind streamliner posed in many publicity photos, and had its likeness rendered in artist Grif Teller's famous portraits of the railroad. In 1940, another four K4s' received slightly more conservative (and more practical) streamlining as shown on page 76.

A number of efforts were made to further improve the K-class design. In 1929, two K5 prototypes were built. While they were very promising, the railroad continued to experiment with the K4 design, modifying it in dozens of ways. For example, two K4s' were equipped with roller bearings, and another three had boosters installed.

Two K4s' are preserved. The 3750 is on display at Strasburg, Pa., while the 1361 sat for many years on public display at Horseshoe Curve. It was restored to operating condition in the 1980s and run on various excursions before being put in indefinite storage.

CLASS L 2-8-2 (MIKADO): When the PRR adopted the 2-8-2 in 1914, the type was already well established. Mikados were first designed by Baldwin in 1897 for use in Japan, and the Northern Pacific had been using them since 1905. The PRR introduced the Class L1s Mikado the same year as the K4s Pacific, and both locomotives employed the same boiler.

The PRR took delivery of 574 L1s Mikados between 1914 and 1919 and used them primarily to replace aging H8 Consolidations in freight service. The L1s burned an enormous amount of fuel, and since most were built before PRR accepted the use of the automatic stoker, which automatically fed coal to the firebox (the first stokers were introduced about 1912), it was not uncommon for the railroad to assign two firemen to L1s on heavy runs. Today, one L1s, No. 520, is preserved at the Railroad Museum of Pennsylvania.

The PRR also had a handful of Mikados that were of USRA (United States Railroad Administration) design dating from World War I when the USRA operated most U.S. railroads. Designated as L2s, these locomotives were unpopular and usually only worked lines west of Pittsburgh.

CLASS M 4-8-2 (MOUNTAIN): In 1923, the PRR introduced a new, dual-service locomotive, the 4-8-2 Mountain type. The first M1, No. 4700, designed and built that year, was based largely on the successful I1s Decapod and, in the tradition of PRR standardization, used many of the same components. After two years of testing, the railroad ordered 200 of them, making for a total of 201 M1's. Some were built at Juniata Shops while others were built by both Baldwin and Lima. They featured 72-inch drivers, 27x30-inch cylinders, weighed nearly 385,000 pounds, and produced 64,500 pounds of tractive force.

The M1 performed well and was liked by both crews and management. The Pennsy was so pleased with the M1 that it ordered another 100, designated M1a, in 1930. Essentially the same as the earlier M1's, the M1a's each featured an additional air compressor, a Worthington feedwater heater, and weighed an additional 5,000 pounds.

After World War II the PRR sought to obtain greater performance from the M1's. In 1946 it upgraded 38 M1a's by increasing their boiler pressure to 270 pounds and modifying their fireboxes to increase the heating surface. The resulting locomotives were designated M1b, and produced an additional 5,000 pound of tractive force.

The M1's were preferred for heavy service in lightly graded territory and were commonly found operating east of Altoona on the Middle Division and the Philadelphia Division, and west of Pittsburgh on the Ft. Wayne and St. Louis divisions. Today the 6755 is preserved at the Railroad Museum of Pennsylvania in Strasburg.

Mountain 6854 drifts along with a freight at an unknown location, probably during the Depression. Although the M1's were designed for dual service, the locomotives worked mostly in heavy freight service. Despite PRR's normally conservative approach toward mechanical gadgetry, all production M1's were equipped with stokers. All of the M1's were superheated, although the railroad chose not to reflect this in their designation (thus no "M1s"). *Cal's Classics*

Class N 2-10-2 (Santa Fe type): The PRR's lines west of Pittsburgh maintained considerable autonomy through the 1920s and had different locomotive practices than the rest of the system. Locomotive tenders were lettered PENNSYLVANIA LINES, rather than just PENNSYLVANIA. Many Lines West locomotives had centered headlights and front mounted bells, rather than standard PRR practice of high-mounted headlights and bells mounted on the boiler behind the smoke stack. During World War I, Lines West designed its own large motive power, 2-10-2 Santa Fe-types designated as N1s. This entire class was contracted out to Alco and Baldwin. Sixty N1s' were delivered in 1918 and 1919. They featured 62-inch drivers, 30x32-inch cylinders, weighed 435,000 pounds, and delivered 84,890 pounds of tractive effort.

Another 130 Santa Fe types, PRR Class N2s, were ordered from Alco and Baldwin by the USRA near the end of World War I. These were of a standard USRA design and lighter than the N1s. The N2s' were unusual because they did not feature PRR's trademark Belpaire firebox, but used radial stay fireboxes instead. The PRR later rebuilt the Class N2s with Belpaires and reclassed them N2sa; it also relocated "misplaced" trappings such as headlights and bells.

The N's were limited to just 35 mph and spent most of their lives hauling heavy mineral trains in Ohio and western Pennsylvania, although some also worked farther east on the Elmira Branch in Upstate New York.

Switchers

The Pennsylvania's vast system relied on an army of switch engines to work its yards, local freights, and industrial spurs. The railroad had three basic classes of switchers: Class A 0-4-0s for light switching, Class B 0-6-0s for general switching, and Class C 0-8-0s for heavy switching and transfer work. Many of the smaller switchers were either saddle-back tank engines, or equipped with small sloping tenders that made it easier for engineers to operate in reverse. All told, the PRR operated more than 250 A-class, more than 1,200 B-class, and roughly 100 C-class switch engines.

Mallets and Articulateds

Many Eastern coal-hauling railroads operated whole fleets of Mallets and, later, simple articulated engines. The Mallet was a compound engine, which reused steam from its trailing set of cylinders in the lead set of cylinders. It is readily identified by very large, low pressure cylinders at the front of the locomotive.

Simple articulated locomotives are essentially two engines using the same boiler, and normally both sets of cylinders are the same size. However, the PRR was not enthralled with the prospect of articulated steam locomotives, although it operated a few of both the Mallet-compound and simple articulated varieties.

Class CC 0-8-8-0 (Mallets): By far the most numerous articulated on the PRR were the eleven CC class. A single CC1 built by Baldwin in 1912 was joined by ten CC2's in 1919. These locomotive were generally used on Lines West and often hauled drag freights or worked as pushers.

Class HC1 2-8-8-0 experimental: In 1919, Juniata Shops built a sole, single-expansion, simple articulated of a very unusual type. It featured an enormous Belpaire boiler, 62-inch drivers, weighed 586,500 pounds, and delivered an incredible 147,640 pounds of tractive effort. Despite its relatively successful design, it

In the steam era, 0-6-0 switchers were a fixture at nearly every PRR yard and industrial area. Here a B-class putts along with a transfer run made up of Pullmans in Chicago circa 1950. *Cal's Classics*

S1 6100 is at the Englewood stop on the south side of Chicago, possibly with the *Broadway Limited*. This one-of-a-kind was scrapped in 1949, but its unique streamlined design has inspired artists and designers for more than 50 years. Its likeness still appears in design books, on posters, record albums, and computer games. *Cal's Classics*

was never duplicated and spent most its short life working as a pusher out of Altoona. It was scrapped around 1930.

CLASS HH 2-8-8-2: In 1911, the PRR received a single Class HH1s 2-8-8-2 simple articulated from Alco. It delivered nearly 100,000 pounds of tractive effort, which was more than the railroad knew how to handle efficiently at the time. It was primarily used in helper service; no more were ordered. During World War II, when the PRR was experiencing a record traffic surge, it acquired six N&W Class Y-3 2-8-8-2 Mallets. The PRR reclassified these as HH1 (no "s"); the sole 1911 machine had been scrapped many years earlier.

Duplexes and Turbines

At the end of the 1920s, when other railroads were ordering new super-powered steam locomotives—those with outside-bearing, two-axle radial trailing trucks designed to carry significantly enlarged fireboxes that could produce sufficient steam at any speed—PRR was content building its more traditional M1a 4-8-2's. Further, during the 1930s the PRR elected to concentrate on its electrification projects rather than design new steam power. As a result, the railroad never owned a large variety of modern, powerful, efficient models which were popular on other lines. There were no Berkshires (2-8-4), Hudsons (4-6-4), or Northerns (4-8-4) on the PRR roster, although during World War II, PRR did build its 2-10-4 Texas-types.

In the late 1930s, the conservative PRR took an abrupt turn in motive-power design and embarked on a curious, but

desperate mission to build the next generation of steam locomotives. Why the sudden change of heart?

The PRR, of course, had lifelong ties with the coal industry; in its day, the PRR carried more coal than any other American railroad, and coal represented a large portion of its traffic base. However, in the mid-1930s, the PRR tested one of Electro-Motive's early passenger diesels. At first the railroad was skeptical, but when it found that the diesels were doing as good a job as PRR's prized steam fleet, the railroad was astonished. Furthermore, the diesel was not burdened with as many fuel stops as steam, and could run well at high speed for extended periods. The PRR realized that unless steps were taken quickly, oil-burning diesels might someday supplant coal-burning steam!

In light of all this, the PRR decided to redesign the reciprocating steam locomotive and build one that could out-perform the diesel invader. The railroad's top officials met with Baldwin, Alco, and Lima and suggested that they join forces with the PRR to produce the next generation of coal-burning locomotive, one that could haul a 14-car loaded passenger train at 100 mph for extended periods with only a few pauses to take on fuel and water. They agreed, and in 1939 a machine unlike anything ever seen before was unveiled. . .

THE CLASS S1 6-4-4-6 DUPLEX: The mammoth 6-4-4-6 Class S1, No. 6100, represented a serious departure from PRR's conventional wisdom, and it came with a hefty price tag: more than $670,000. It weighed 608,170 pounds and with its tender was 140 feet long. It featured two pairs

With their shark-nose styling, there was no mistaking Pennsy's T1's. The 5507 is wheeling eastbound with the *Admiral* at Junction Tower in Fort Wayne. The date is August 18, 1948. By this time, the problem-prone T1s had been bumped to less prestigious assignments; some were even briefly used in freight service. The T1's were retired several years before the end of the steam era, outlived by more traditional locomotives such as the K4s which the T1 had been intended to replace. *R. D. Acton Sr.*

of enormous 84-inch drivers. Its streamlined shrouds were designed by renowned industrial designer Raymond Loewy. The S1 was intended as a replacement for the K4s on heavy, long-haul passenger trains west of Harrisburg. In 1939 and 1940, the railroad awed the public with its super locomotive running stationary on rollers at the New York World's Fair.

Despite its impressive pulling power—more than 71,000 pounds of tractive effort—the S1 was essentially a failure. While it could pull heavy trains at high speed, it had two downfalls. Its designers failed to learn one of the lessons that doomed many radical designs of the past: the locomotive was too big for the railroad's existing plant. Because of its size, the S1 was essentially relegated to the far western end of the system where curves were at a minimum. Its other big failure was its need for very high maintenance. While the S1's tenure was short-lived, it did provide a test bed for the following locomotive class.

CLASS T1 DUPLEX: The T1, PRR's last mass-produced passenger locomotive, inspired a generation of speculation

regarding the viability of the steam locomotive. This sleek, streamlined speedster was truly PRR's response to the diesel-electric. A combination of lighter reciprocating parts, shorter cylinder stroke, and non-articulated rigid frame gave the Duplex a decided advantage in the eyes of Pennsylvania management.

Two prototype T1's, Nos. 6110 and 6111, were delivered by Baldwin in 1942. They featured shark-nosed styling by Raymond Loewy and were painted in Pennsy's businesslike Brunswick green, accented by stripes and large red keystones on the pilot and tenders. Essentially a scaled down, refined S1, the T1 had 80-inch drivers and weighed in at 497,200 pounds. With its exceptionally large, eight-axle, streamlined Class 180-P-84 tender, the T1 was 122 feet long. It produced 65,000 pounds of tractive effort, more than 6,000 horsepower when running faster than 55 mph, and could operate effortlessly at speeds over 100 mph for extended periods.

The railroad was pleased with the T1's performance at the Altoona test plant and ordered 50 production T1 locomotives from

Altoona and from Baldwin; they were delivered in 1945 and 1946. The T1's entered passenger service as intended, west of Harrisburg and replaced pairs of K4s on the railroad's crack passenger trains.

The T1's reign was very short. Even before the first production engines were in service, PRR had ordered a pair of Electro-Motive E7 passenger diesels. When the T1 began to develop problems—one of which was that the locomotives tended to slip at speed—the railroad was cautious about further investments. The cost savings provided by the T1's thoroughly superior performance was quickly eaten up by higher maintenance costs, particularly on its valvework. Ultimately, diesels prevailed. Even the steam-minded PRR could no longer ignore the diesel's cost-savings effectiveness.

Q1 AND Q2 DUPLEX: The Pennsylvania's solution to modern freight steam was the unorthodox Duplexes, Class Q1 and Q2. The Q1, No. 6131, was an experimental 4-6-4-4 non-articulated type. It was particularly unusual because its second set of 77-inch drivers were powered by rear-facing cylinders placed beneath the firebox. It was originally streamlined, although in later years much of its shrouding was removed. With its trailing-truck booster, the Q1 could generate 90,000 pounds of tractive effort. The Q1 had many problems, but the PRR went on to perfect the design, developing the Q2, 4-4-6-4 Duplex type.

In 1944 and 1945, Altoona outshopped 25 Q2's. Unlike the Q1, all of the Q2's four cylinders faced forward. They featured smaller drivers than the Q1, only 69 inches, and weighed a phenomenal 619,100 pounds. It was one of the most powerful reciprocating steam locomotives ever built, generating more than 115,000 pounds of tractive effort. Like the T1, its operation proved problematic and its career short-lived. Most of them were withdrawn from service in 1949.

CLASS S2 6-4-6 STEAM TURBINE: PRR's other hope for continuing the coal-powered locomotive was the steam turbine. GE built a coal-fired turbine-electric for Union Pacific in 1938, and in 1944 Baldwin delivered to the PRR a unique 6-4-4-6 direct-drive steam turbine Class S2, No. 6200. Whereas the GE turbine resembled a diesel, Baldwin's looked like a steam locomotive, although without cylinders and drive rods. In their place was a direct (geared) turbine drive which engaged the second and third driving axles. Traditional side-rods connected all the drive wheels.

The S2 weighed 589,920 pounds, featured 68-inch drivers, and delivered 70,500 pounds tractive effort. It rode well, and was very powerful. It was used in both freight and passenger service, drawing such prestige assignments as the *Broadway Limited* and inspiring famous toy train manufacturer Lionel to produce an interpretive model of it. The S2's downfall was fuel consumption and high maintenance. The PRR had planned to build a Class V1 turbine-electric as a follow-on to the S2, but canceled it and ordered diesels instead.

Q2 6197 was one of 25 of this class, built by Altoona. The Q-class was to be the next generation of modern steam, but most of the monsters had been sidelined less than five years after they were outshopped. The PRR was finally coming to terms that dieselization was inevitable. *Cal's Classics*

Behemoths of PRR's electric fleet abound on an impressive merchandise freight rolling along the Northeast Corridor route (New York-Washington) on a fair autumn day in 1966. A closer look reveals that the pantographs of the two GG1's are down, an indication that they're only along for the ride and E44 No. 4428 is doing all the work. Pennsy's "motor" roster featured many models of many types, but during the railroad's twilight years, the E44 and certainly the time-proven GG1 were the mainstay of electric locomotion for freight and passengers. *Hank Goerke*

Electric Locomotives of the PRR

AMERICA'S LARGEST FLEET OF ELECTRIC MOTIVE POWER

At the turn of the century when the Pennsylvania Railroad decided to build a terminal in Manhattan and connect it with tunnels beneath the Hudson and East rivers, it knew that electric locomotives would have to be used to haul its trains. So, in typical PRR fashion, the railroad began extensive testing of electric locomotives in preparation for its Pennsylvania Station operations.

The New York Terminal was no small deed, and the railroad wanted to design the best locomotive possible for its boldest adventure. When the PRR designed a new class of steam locomotive, it thoroughly tested every aspect of the new device before mass-producing it for revenue service. PRR's foray in the new field of electric locomotives exemplified this philosophy. For additional insight to the electric side of the PRR, be sure you've read Chapter 5.

Early Electrics 1905 to 1924

Early on, the PRR planned to employ direct-current third-rail distribution on its Pennsylvania Station project, and the first experimental electrics were constructed accordingly. In 1905, PRR's Juniata Shops built two experimental electrics, Nos. 10001 and 10002, using Westinghouse electrical equipment. Each locomotive featured a different traction-motor configuration, but both locomotives employed an articulated B-B wheel arrangement. (Electric locomotive wheel arrangements use a number to designate unpowered wheel sets, and letters to indicated powered sets; an "A" represents one powered wheel set, "B," two powered wheel sets, and so on. For example, a 2-D-2 would have two unpowered wheel sets, four driving wheel sets, and two more unpowered sets.)

Initially 10001 and 10002 were tested on a short section of the Long Island Rail Road that had been electrified in preparation for the terminal project. The two locomotives demonstrated severe tracking problems, leading PRR engineers to re-examine steam-locomotive designs and also borrow an electric locomotive from neighbor New Haven for evaluation.

The PRR then ordered a third experimental electric, No. 10003, from Baldwin/Westinghouse in 1907. This 70-ton, rigid-frame locomotive featured 72-inch drivers in a 2-B wheel arrangement—identical to the popular 4-4-0 configuration used on American-type steam locomotives. Unlike the two previous experimentals, this locomotive was designed to operate from an 11,000-volt alternating current overhead electrification system such as that used by the New Haven. Of the three experimentals, the 10003 was by far the most desirable and it was used as the basis for the successful DD1 locomotive design.

CLASS DD1 SIDE-ROD ELECTRIC: In 1909, Juniata Shops built a DD1 prototype, No. 3998. This electric locomotive was comprised of two semi-permanently coupled units, each 65 feet long, weighing 313,000

Two P5's have a grip on an apparently endless unit coal train on the Trenton Cutoff in 1962. These were the heaviest, most powerful of the PRR's three box-cab designs, and ultimately the most successful, relatively speaking. Although initially intended for passenger service, design flaws led to the P5's being regeared and relegated to freight service. *John Dziobko*

pounds featuring 72-inch drivers in 2-B wheel arrangement. Each unit was powered by a single, powerful traction motor connected to the drivers through a series of rods and jack shafts. The PRR had anticipated the need for great power, since the DD1's would have to haul 800-ton trains of steel passenger cars up 1.8 percent grades in the Hudson River tunnels (see page 62).

The railroad was extremely pleased with the DD1's performance and built a second prototype in the spring of 1910, No. 3999. At the time these were among the most powerful locomotives in the world, delivering an amazing 80,000 pounds of tractive force. Yet, the DD1's performance was not measured simply by its brute power; they were fast, too—capable of 85 mph.

The PRR made a few minor adjustments to DD1 design before building 31 additional pairs. Juniata Shops built all of the DD1's at a cost of $53,347 per pair. The DD1's were worth every penny and demonstrated their exceptional design on a daily

basis. By the middle teens, the 33 DD1 pairs were handling roughly 600 daily trains in and out of Pennsylvania Station. They operated exclusively on the 14 miles of electrified main line between Sunnyside Yard and Manhattan Transfer, an isolated station in the Jersey Meadows where electric power was exchanged for steam.

The DD1 fleet enjoyed a long productive career, despite their limited service area. They were renumbered into double digits, carrying the numbers 10 to 42. In the late 1920s, when the newer L5a's bumped many DD1s from trans-Hudson assignments, a number of DD1s were transferred to the LIRR where they served in commuter service for another 25 years.

By the late 1940s, the PRR began scrapping surplus DD1's, and the LIRR had disposed of all of its DD1's by 1952. However a few soldiered on; set 39-36 continued to operate into the 1960s. Today, this beautifully restored pair is at the Railroad Museum of Pennsylvania.

The big locomotive, nicknamed "Big Liz," was never duplicated, and PRR eventually shifted the emphasis of its electrification from the Alleghenies to the Northeast Corridor. Big Liz found work as the Paoli pusher where it worked until about 1940, when it was scrapped.

CLASS L5 SIDE-ROD ELECTRICS: The PRR built a single L5-class electric locomotive for a.c. overhead electric service in 1924. It featured a 1-D-1 wheel arrangement. It was not nearly as powerful as Big Liz and was known to crews as "Little Jenny."

Between 1924 and 1926, the PRR built 23 L5a electrics which were similar to the lone L5 except that they ran on d.c. third rail and thus served exclusively on the New York Terminal electrification. These new machines were bigger and more powerful than the DD1's and largely replaced them on passenger runs into Pennsylvania Station. After the Manhattan electrification was converted to overhead a.c. operation in 1933, most of the L5's became surplus. All of were scrapped during World War II.

Switchers

In 1926, the PRR began building three-axle electric switch engines that essentially emulated the successful 0-6-0 steam switcher. Initially these locomotives were operated in pairs and classed BB1 and BB2; later the pairs were separated and each locomotive reclassed B1. The PRR had constructed 28 of the diminutive box cabs by 1935. For years they worked Sunnyside Yard and Pennsylvania Station, Philadelphia's Broad Street, and other yards in the electrified territory (see page 64). A handful of B1's survived into the 1960s, and one is preserved at Strasburg.

Later Box-Cabs

Westinghouse introduced a vastly improved traction motor in 1927 which was small enough to fit between the locomotive wheels and therefore obviate the need for the rod and jack-shaft arrangement typical on early electrics. This innovation changed the way the PRR thought about electrification and greatly influenced its decision to electrify more than 200 miles of its main lines. In 1930 and 1931 the PRR designed and built three new classes of box-cab electrics: L6, O1, and P5. While all looked very similar, they dif-

FF1 SIDE-ROD ELECTRIC: In one of its early electrification schemes, the PRR considered stringing wires all the way to Pittsburgh. For such a service it would need powerful electric locomotives to haul heavy freights, and in 1917 Juniata Shops built a single FF1 prototype, No. 3931. At more than 76 feet long and 258 tons heavy, and with six pairs of 72-inch drivers in a 1-C+C-1 wheel arrangement, this locomotive was truly a monster. This curious side-rod, jack-shaft-powered, box-cab was the railroad's first true overhead-electric-fed locomotive.

The railroad wanted a powerful locomotive, and that's what it got. The FF1 produced 88,000 pounds of continuous tractive effort (roughly equivalent to a I1s Decapod), however it could produce a tremendous 140,000 pounds starting-tractive effort, roughly 7,500 hp. This was an enormous amount of power in 1917 (and still is even by today's standards)—too much for the lightly built equipment of the time. In test runs it reportedly pulled out couplers.

fered in their wheel arrangement, weight, tractive effort, and intended service. True to PRR standardization, these three classes shared common parts.

CLASS L6 (2-D-2): Two 2-D-2 L6's were constructed at Altoona, with Westinghouse and GE electrical components. They were originally intended for heavy freight service, but after a few years were relegated to Pennsylvania Station switching service.

The railroad ordered a fleet of 50 L6a's from Lima, and 30 carbodies were constructed. However a radical shift in PRR's electric-locomotive philosophy, stemming from problems with the rigid-frame box-cab design and other aspects of the P5 design, caused the railroad to cancel the L6 order after just one was completed.

CLASS O1 (2-B-2): Eight O1 box-cabs of four different subclasses—O1, O1a, O1b, and O1c—were built at Altoona. All O1's had a 2-B-2 wheel arrangement, but each subclass employed different electrical equipment, varied slightly in output, and featured minor external differences. The O1's were intended as the primary electric haulers of light passenger trains, but proved underpowered when operated individually. The PRR tended to use them in pairs on short-distance passenger runs, and they were often assigned to Lehigh Valley passenger trains between Newark and New York's Pennsylvania Station.

CLASS P5 (2-C-2): In 1931 the PRR built two prototype P5 box-cabs featuring a 2-C-2 wheel arrangement. They weighed 392,000 pounds (roughly the same as an M1a Mountain type), and produced 3,730 hp. and 55,000 pounds starting tractive effort. The railroad was satisfied with the initial performance of these feisty electrics and ordered 90 production models, classed P5a. Some were built at Altoona, others by either Baldwin or Lima.

The P5 class were designed as heavy passenger locomotives, and it appeared as if the P5a's would indeed provide the PRR with all the passenger power it required on the newly electrified New York-Philadelphia route (see page 67). On January 16, 1933, a shining new P5 led its first intercity electric passenger train. It departed Broad Street in Philadelphia amidst pomp and circumstance. However the P5's soon revealed design flaws.

The P5's and other box-cabs displayed serious tracking difficulties at speed. Also, while the P5's could easily handle trains up to ten cars singly, longer consists required costly doubleheading. Then more severe problems surfaced. The P5's began developing cracks in their driving axles, which sidelined many of the units. The PRR brought in its reliable K4s Pacifics—recently displaced by the electrification—to substitute for the ailing electrics.

Then tragedy struck, forever altering the fate of PRR's box-cab fleet. On a wintery day in January 1934, P5a 4772 struck a heavy truck at a grade crossing in Deans, N.J. The P5's head-end crew riding in the unprotected box-cab was killed. The immediate consequence was that the remaining 28 P5a's on order were redesigned. Instead of the box-cab design they were delivered with a streamlined center-cab carbody and designated "P5a modified."

Ultimately the P5 fleet was regeared and relegated to freight service. They operated until the early 1960s when most were retired on the delivery of the E44 electrics. Prototype 4700 is today displayed at the National Museum of Transport in St. Louis.

CLASS GG1 (2-C+C-2): Pennsylvania Railroad's GG1 electric was one of the most impressive pieces of railroad equipment to roll on American rails. Its perfect aesthetics, tremendous pulling power, unparalleled acceleration, and longevity made the GG1 a legend in its own time.

In 1933 when its P5a developed serious flaws, the PRR again borrowed one of New Haven's state-of-the-art box-cab electrics to test, this time a 1931 vintage EP-3a. This locomotive differed from the P5a and all other PRR electrics in that it featured an articulated chassis. Furthermore, it distributed its power over six driving axles in a 2-C+C-2 wheel arrangement (the plus [+] sign indicating articulation) rather than

The 4770 at Enola in 1962 represents the "P5a modified" and at the time was the last modified P5a in operation. The overall carbody style of these later P5's was the forerunner of the GG1. *William Volkmer*

just three driving axles as did the P5a.

PRR mechanical engineers were impressed and arranged to have Baldwin and GE build a streamlined locomotive based on the EP-3a design. At the same time, they also had Baldwin and Westinghouse construct a rigid-chassis electric of the railroad's own design, essentially an enlarged version of the P5a featuring a 2-D-2 wheel arrangement. The two locomotives, respectively designated GG1 and R1, were completed in 1934. Both locomotives had similar, safety-inspired center-cab, streamlined carbodies.

The first GG1, No. 4899, was 79.5 feet long, had 12 motors, was geared for 100 mph, and rated at 4,620 hp. The R1 was only 64.7 feet long, had 8 motors, was likewise geared for a 100 mph, and rated at 5,000 hp. After test-track examinations, the two prototypes were raced up and down the main line. After careful scrutiny, the GG1 was found to be the superior locomotive. It was re-numbered 4800, and an

order for 57 similar locomotives was split between Baldwin, GE, and Altoona.

The PRR hired Raymond Loewy, one of the nation's best known industrial designers, to refine the GG1's streamlined carbody. (It is often mistakenly believed that Loewy provided the overall design for the GG1 carbody; he did not.) Loewy suggested using an all-welded carbody, such as those being built for automobiles, and he also adjusted minor styling details. One of the most remembered aspects of his treatment were the famous five gold pin stripes, known as "cat whiskers," which nicely augmented the locomotive's stately Brunswick green paint (see back cover photo). These stripes, which held the contour of the locomotive, were later added to many PRR locomotives. Many non-railroad machines, including tractor-trailer trucks and vacuum cleaners would later display variations of the Loewy pin stripes.

The sleek, streamlined, and now all-welded GG1 was in good company in the

The GG1 was universally popular among railroaders, the traveling public, and railroad enthusiasts. Untold thousands of children learned to appreciate the sublime wonders of modern railroading when they received Lionel's O-gauge replica of Pennsy's original. And tens of millions of travelers rode behind the GG1 during its nearly 50-year reign on the Northeast Corridor. Two of the revered locomotives lead an Army-Navy game train at Philadelphia in 1963. *John Dziobko*

mid-1930s. Streamlining was all the rage, and other railroads had also introduced radical, modern-looking streamlined trains. The Burlington had its *Zephyr*, the Union Pacific its M-10000 *City of Salina*, and now the PRR had its mighty GG1.

Streamlining conveyed speed, and the GG1 did not just look fast, it *was* fast. It could accelerate from zero to 100 mph in a little more than a minute. It could maintain 100-mph speeds with a loaded train continuously without straining, and in early tests it reached 115 mph. In later years, the GG1 would attain speeds of up to 128 mph.

The first production GG1, No. 4840, arrived in August 1935, and soon the new "G's" had bumped the troubled P5a's from premier assignments between New York and Washington. The railroad was very pleased with the new locomotives' performance. The GG1's exemplary acceleration enabled the PRR to trim schedules, and they could easily handle even long passenger trains, taking 18-20 cars without strain and eliminating costly double heading. When the railroad planned to extend its electrification from to Harrisburg, it ordered more GG1s, and on January 15, 1938, a shining G led the first electrically-powered train in to Pennsylvania's capital city.

The PRR continued to order GG1s, even after it had tested other designs, notably the 2-B+B-2 DD2. By 1943, the railroad had amassed a fleet of 139 GG1's, including the original prototype, 4800, which was affectionately known as "Rivets."

In their early years, PRR assigned the GG1's almost exclusively to passenger trains, allowing the P5's and various experimental units to handle freight in electrified territory. However, in their later years the G's often saw freight service. In that capacity, they were often operated in pairs.

Over the years Pennsylvania's GG1s wore a number of paint schemes, mostly variations on the Loewy-inspired striping. During the war years and into the early 1950s, though, there were no significant changes in the livery; Brunswick Green and gold pin stripes suited the railroad just fine. However, 1952 brought a bold aesthetical improvement. Several GG1s were repainted in PRR's trademark Tuscan red along with traditional gold striping for use on Budd-built stainless-steel streamlined

consists assigned to the *Senator* and the *Congressional* (page 74). In 1955, the PRR introduced a new "simplified" standard paint scheme on the GG1's consisting of a single broad stripe, larger lettering, and very large red keystones. Also about this time, three GG1's received all-silver livery with a red stripe. The intended assignments for these silver G's were the stainless-steel trains, and only wore this peculiar paint scheme for a very short time.

The GG1's were exceptionally durable machines; their tough frames were virtually indestructible. Even when involved in collisions, the GG1 nearly always triumphed. One of the most spectacular crashes of the 1950s involved GG1 4876, a January 1939 graduate of Altoona Works.

In the early morning hours of January 15, 1953, the 4876 was leading a tardy *Federal*, a through train from Boston, down the Northeast Corridor toward Washington. This morning, engineer Harry Brower was at the throttle of 4876 which had replaced a New Haven motor at New York. As he approached Washington Union Station, Brower found the train did not have needed braking capacity to slow down. He dumped the air, yet the train kept right on rolling. All efforts to stop the speeding train proved futile, as it was heading downgrade toward the terminal! As the train bore down on the stub-end station tracks, engineer Brower leaned on the horn (remember, this was in the days before on-train radio communication). The GG1 was screaming like a banshee as it raced toward peril. A quick-thinking tower operator phoned the station to alert all of the runaway. Pennsylvania 4876 with the *Federal* in tow made an unforgettable grand entrance into Union Station at 35 mph, smashing through the bumping post, the stationmaster's office, a newspaper stand, and into the concourse. The GG1's tremendous weight was far more than the concourse floor could withstand, and before the dust had settled, 4876 collapsed into the basement.

Engineer Brower suffered minor injuries and another 86 people on board the train were hurt, but no one was killed. The aftermath of the wreck led to phenomenal photos in papers all around the nation, and for a moment, 4876 was the railroad's most famous locomotive. Cleaning up the mess was another story. The 4876 was cut into sections and sent to Altoona. Ten months later it re-emerged like a phoenix, now wearing a fresh coat of Tuscan red paint. This durable locomotive served faithfully for another 30 years, a testimony to the GG1's superior design.

A few of PRR's older GG1's were retired in the late 1960s, but most survived the 1968 Penn Central merger. GG1's survived into the 1980s; the last run of a G was on an excursion on October 29, 1983. Since that time, many of the famous electrics have been preserved and restored. Two GG1s, including Rivets, are on display at Strasburg, and other G's can be seen at Harrisburg, Elkhart, Ind., Green Bay, Wis., and Union, Ill., among other places. Even the celebrated runaway 4876 survives.

Late Electrics

E2B/E3B/E3C: In the early 1950s, the PRR looked toward replacing its P5a fleet with a new generation of electric locomotives. Ten experimental units were built: four E2b's by GE, and four E3b's and two E3c's by Westinghouse-Baldwin-Lima. Externally, all three models resembled carbody diesel-electric locomotives of the period. The E2's were four-axle locomotives using a standard B-B wheel arrangement. Each unit developed 2,500 hp. using conventional electric-locomotive design. The E3's employed a radical new technology which used ignitron-rectifier tubes to convert the high-voltage (11,000-volt) a.c. from the overhead catenary to 600-volt d.c. power for traction motors similar to those in conventional diesel-electrics. The E3b rode on an unorthodox three-truck two-axle wheel arrangement, while the E3c featured a two-truck, six-axle arrangement. The PRR studied these new designs for several years but delayed purchasing a new electric fleet, instead focusing on diesels.

CLASS F2 (1-C+C-1): A freight traffic surge in 1956 interrupted PRR's locomotive plans. As a result, steam survived a few seasons longer than expected and there was increased pressure on the aging electric fleet. To cope with the sudden rise in traffic, the railroad picked up secondhand a.c. box-cabs from the Great Northern.

Having retired its Cascade Tunnel electrification, GN gave PRR a good price on its eight 1-C+C-1 electrics, built between 1927 and 1930. Seven, Nos. 1-7, became PRR Class FF2 and were quickly pressed into service (one was held for parts). They were used primarily as freight helpers.

CLASS E44 (C-C): The antique, secondhand FF's were just a stopgap measure to handle the swell in freight traffic. The PRR was weighing the costs its electric operations versus that of diesel-electric locomotives and at the time decided that electrics were indeed superior to diesel. It ordered new E44 electrics based largely on research from the early 1950s experimentals and the success of the E33 ignitron rectifier locomotives built by GE for the Virginian Railway in 1956.

Between 1960 and 1963, the PRR took delivery of its last new electric locomotives, 66 4,400-hp E44's built by GE. The boxy locomotives employed six powered axles in a C-C wheel arrangement. The first E44's used ignitron tubes much like those used in the E33's, but later E44's employed more modern silicon rectifiers instead. As the E44's came on line, the PRR gradually retired all of its P5a's and most of the oddball electrics, including the FF2's.

The E44's were designed as heavy freight haulers and spent most of their careers in freight service. They were used on freights all over the electrified lines. However on rare occasions they were called to haul passenger trains. Since the E44's were geared for only 70 mph, they were not well-suited for service on the high-speed Northeast Corridor. Illustration of these beefy units can be seen in chapter 7.🚂

An E3b and an E3C mingle, coupled, at Enola engine terminal in June 1962. Though built as pairs, the units operated singly or with other electrics. The E3b featured an unusual B-B-B wheel arrangement while the E3c utilized a more-conventional C-C wheel arrangement. As experimentals, the locomotives were quite expensive. *William Volkmer*

Pennsy's large fleet of "sharknose" freight and passenger diesels, built by Baldwin Locomotive Works of Eddystone, Pa., were among the road's most-distinctive diesels. Their rakish lines made them look like they were dashing along, even when in fact they were parked. Between 1949 and 1952, the PRR purchased 170 freight sharks, such as the 9595 recorded on Kodachrome at Kinsman Yard in Cleveland in 1958. They operated into the 1960s. *Richard J. Solomon*

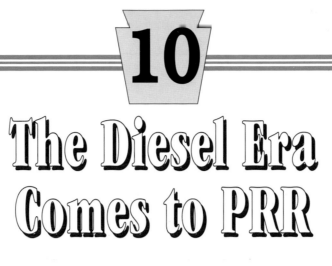

10

The Diesel Era Comes to PRR

AN ECLECTIC ARMY OF DIESELS SUPPLANT STEAM

The Pennsylvania Railroad until the 1940s was firmly committed to the steam locomotive. It wasn't that the PRR thought that diesels didn't perform well; it was the prospect that nationwide dieselization threatened PRR's coal traffic. Yet, despite PRR's attachment to steam and its heroic effort to promote the technology, the economies of diesel operation eventually convinced the railroad to abandon steam.

Despite PRR's steam loyalties, internal-combustion power made an early appearance on the PRR. The railroad acquired its first true diesel locomotive in 1937, a 600-hp. SW switcher from Electro-Motive Corp. It was an experiment, an exception to the rule, and for several years it remained an isolated curiosity among the nation's largest fleet of steam and electric locomotives. When EMC introduced its FT diesel in 1939, often considered the locomotive which proved that diesels were worthy freight haulers, the PRR was not interested.

However, by 1947, when the PRR had caved in to dieselization, it began to acquire new diesel-electrics at an unprecedented rate, acting like a crazed, sugar-deprived kid in a candy shop. The PRR bought every sort of diesel imaginable, from every builder—freight cabs, passenger cabs, switchers, road-switchers, and transfer locomotives. It bought from Baldwin, Alco, Electro-Motive (Electro-Motive Division of General Motors, or EMD, after 1941), Lima-Hamilton, General Electric,

and Fairbanks-Morse. It sampled, it tasted, and it munched away. Within a short time it had thousands of units and maintained the most diverse, eclectic fleet of diesels in the world.

It was an odd policy for a railroad that for 80 years had taken great pride in its fleet of standardized steam (and later electric) motive power. Alexander Cassatt must have twirled in his grave when he realized what the PRR had done in its ravenous acquisition of different diesels. While this made motive-power watching on the PRR fascinating, it was in some cases a disaster for the railroad.

In PRR's eagerness to acquire new diesel-electrics, it had sacrificed one of the advantages that diesel power provided: greatly reduced maintenance costs. Since each brand of locomotive required its own parts supply, and in some cases different models of the same brand required their own parts, the PRR had to maintain six different supply networks. Traction motors, engine blocks, even wheels were different. There were other difficulties too. A mechanic who worked on two-stroke EMD prime-movers might not know how to repair a four-stroke Alco. Nor would locomotives of different manufactures necessarily work together in multiple.

PRR did achieve some savings over steam by using diesels. However had it purchased fewer model types, its operating department would have experienced far less grief, and the railroad would have achieved a much greater savings from its investment. Even with its drive to achieve complete dieselization, the PRR was among the last big railroads in the East to run steam. By the time the PRR merged with New York Central in 1968, it had acquired 3,083 diesel-electric locomotives.

Initially PRR painted all of its diesels Brunswick green (a very dark green, that appears black in most color photographs). Some of its cab units received Raymond Loewy's gold "cat whiskers" like those applied to the GG1 electrics, while others receive a single thin stripe. The switchers and road-switchers were adorned in even more Spartan paint. Initially other lines dressed their diesels in fancy colors, but not the conservative PRR. However, beginning in the early 1950s, some passenger locomotives were painted Tuscan red with the pin stripes. More distinctive of PRR's diesel fleet was not its paint schemes, but the large radio antennas that ran the length of most road units.

In addition to the builder's model classifications, the PRR developed a class system of its own. Every class of locomotive was identified by a letter and number combination that indicated its builder, intended service, and horsepower rating. Thus an Alco model FA1 cab unit was designated Class AF15 (Alco, freight, 1,500 hp.) on the PRR.

Because nearly every diesel model that PRR bought was an "off the shelf" catalog model and not unique to the Pennsy per se, we'll dispense with the specifics of each model—information that can be obtained from any number of general books on diesel-electric locomotives. To further simplify coverage, most of PRR's various diesel classes will only be handled in broad terms; for example, "BF" for Baldwin road-freight diesels. For more information on subclasses (e.g., "BF15a"), we recommend the PENNSY POWER series books authored and published by Alvin F. Staufer.

Alco

CLASSES AS AND ARS: The PRR operated 516 Alco diesels of 23 different models. The PRR owned a large fleet of Alco switchers, mostly S2's, S4's and a handful of T-6's, all grouped in the AS class. The 115 RS3's were the most common Alco variety on the PRR, grouped as ARS (Alco road-switcher) including 45 with steam generators for passenger service.

CLASS AFP: Perhaps one of its most interesting fleets of Alcos were the ten PA and five PB units. This was one of the more

Two Alco cousins, an RSD15 and an RSD12, team up to push a freight up the mountain out of Altoona during the summer of 1966. These six-axle brutes, PRR Class ARS18a and ARS24 respectively, and their kin were primarily used in pusher service until bumped by newer EMD diesels circa 1967. *John Dziobko*

versatile fleets of PA's. When delivered in 1947, the PA's were first given premier passenger assignments. Soon they were assigned to dual service and often worked freight and secondary passenger trains. By the mid 1950s, the PA's could be found on New York & Long Branch commuter runs, where they relieved GG1's at the then-end of electrification at South Amboy for the run to Bay Head. Other PA's found work as helpers on the Elmira Branch. The PA's were not as successful as their EMD passenger cab counterparts; they only outlasted steam by a few years, and in 1962 they were retired and traded back to Alco for an order of 15 RS27 road-switchers.

CLASS AF: Alco's four-axle FA freight cabs were a little more successful than the PA's. PRR owned 16 FA/FB1's (Class AF15) and 36 FA/FB2's (Class AF16).

Pennsylvania's RS27 fleet (Class AF24) was fairly unusual, as the railroad bought more than half of Alco's entire production run. The chop-nose 2,400-hp. RS27 was an interim model in Alco's catalog, replaced when Alco introduced its Century series in 1963. The PRR operated its fair share of Centurys too: a sole C424 (Class AF24a) was delivered in 1963, followed by 31 C425's in 1964 and 1965, 15 six-axle

C628's in 1965, and 15 six-axle C630's. PRR ordered 3,600 hp C636's from Alco, but they were delivered after the Penn Central merger.

Baldwin

By the time PRR bought its first diesel from Baldwin, the two companies had been doing business for nearly 100 years, therefore it was only natural that the railroad would order Baldwin diesels. Initially PRR gave Baldwin 25 percent of its diesel business, purchasing switchers and road-switchers along with some of the most intriguing diesels ever built: the articulated Centipedes and peculiar-looking "shark-nose" cab locomotives.

The PRR purchased 643 Baldwin diesels, roughly 10 percent of Baldwin's total diesel production. However, as Bald-

TOP: Alco's PA passenger diesels were favorites among diesel connoisseurs. The PRR rostered 15 of them, ten cabs and five boosters, PRR Class AFP20. This back-to-back set is heading west out of Dayton, Ohio, with the *American* on May 23, 1948. *R. D. Acton Sr.* ABOVE: Most of Alco's short-lived RS27 model was purchased by the PRR. One of them leads a GE and two EMD's on a transfer freight in Chicago in 1967. *Jim Boyd*

BELOW: With so many wheels, the "Centipede" nickname was a natural for Baldwin's leviathan DR-12-8-1500/2 diesels. PRR's 24 units originally were delivered semi-permanently coupled. Each unit had a 2-D+D-2 wheel arrangement, a first (and last) for dieseldom. A pair of the babyfaced units sweeps through the Ohio countryside near Manchester in April 1952 with the eastbound *American*. *R. D. Acton Sr.* RIGHT: PRR was the only railroad to buy the sharknose passenger version of Baldwin's DR-6-4-20 diesel model. The 27 Pennsy units (18 cab units, 9 boosters) were built in 1948 and retired early in the 1960s. *John Dziobko*

win diesels developed a reputation for having high maintenance costs and low service availability, the railroad's orders tapered off. The 120-year old Baldwin was struggling to stay in the locomotive business and counted on a few steady customers to pull it through. In 1956, PRR planned to finally retire its last steam engines and place a large order of new diesels. Baldwin bid, anticipating its share of business from its lifelong loyal customer. However, it was not to be. The PRR was feeling financial pressures, and when EMD gave the railroad a good deal on new, reliable GP9's, the PRR sent EMD most of its business. Baldwin management was stunned by this decision, and they appealed to PRR to reconsider. The railroad stood firm, turning its back on the builder that had faithfully built thousands of its locomotives over the years. For Baldwin this was not just a lost bid, it was the end of the line. Baldwin closed most of its vast Eddystone plant and never built another locomotive.

THE BS CLASS included all B-B-truck Baldwin switchers built between 1942 and 1956 of which the PRR bought 385 units, including a dozen for subsidiary PRSL. They were

used systemwide for yard duties and local switching, such as illustrated at the top of page 86.

CLASS BF: Although several railroads bought Baldwin's four-axle freight cab units with the distinctive "sharknose" styling, the PRR owned the largest fleet them—170 units. Like other cab units, they were not well-suited for switching and tended to work through freights.

CLASS BRS: The "RS" designation was for "road-switchers," which are general-purpose units that can be used on road freight, passenger trains, transfer service, or for switching. The PRR had 71 in the BRS group (22 for PRSL), in both four- and six-axle variety; some were equipped with steam generators for passenger service as illustrated in the photo on page 61. The group included 23 unusual 2,400-hp., six-motor center-cab units.

LEFT: Electro-Motive F-units, including an F7A and F7B in Brunswick green and an FP7A in Tuscan, bask in the hazy August sun at East Altoona in 1956. Pennsy went for EMD F's in a big way, ordering 364 units. On the PRR, they were in the EF and EPF class. *John Dziobko*

CLASS BP20: These were one of the few diesels unique to the PRR as the only fleet of A-1-A (six-axle, center axle unpowered) passenger sharks ever built. Baldwin's sharknose styling was in fact based on the design of PRR's T1 Duplex and both the freight and passenger sharks may have been the only diesel to inherit its styling from a steam locomotive.

Baldwin built 18 BP20 cab units, and nine boosters (cabless) in 1948, and they were initially operated west of Harrisburg on long-distance passenger trains. In their early years the passenger sharks were frequent visitors on the Panhandle Division. Later some were regeared and placed in freight service while others wound out their careers in commuter service on the NY&LB.

CLASS BP60: Without a doubt the Baldwin Centipede was one of the most unusual diesel locomotives ever built, and the PRR was one of only three North American railroads to buy them. Twenty-four semi-permanently coupled units (12 pairs) were delivered in 1947 and 1948 intended for passenger service. The PRR assigned them to premier passenger trains, including the *Broadway Limited*. Each Centipede had four 8-cylinder prime movers, and generated 3,000 hp., thus giving a married set 6,000 hp.

The centipedes were quickly discovered to be unreliable and prone to road failures. They had faulty electrical and lubrication

systems which often led to disastrous engine fires. As a result, the Centipedes were down-rated and reclassed as BH50 helpers. For ten years they worked as Altoona pushers and were daily visitors through Horseshoe Curve. In 1958, several were assigned to drag service between Altoona and Enola, and at least one set worked as the Paoli pusher. The Centipedes were withdrawn from service in the early 1960s and most were scrapped by 1964.

Electro-Motive

CLASS EP: Initially the PRR viewed Electro-Motive as a threat and held EMD's entrance into the locomotive market with disdain. However, in 1945 PRR agreed to

ABOVE: One of the most popular diesels to roll on U.S. rails was the GP7/GP9, an all-purpose road-switcher adept at handling just about any assignment. PRR had 376 "Geeps" in its ERS group. At Toledo in 1966, a GP9 and a cabless GP9 booster lead a freight. Like most Eastern lines, PRR operated its high-hood road-switchers long-end forward. *Hank Goerke*

EMD GP30's had an unmistakable look all their own, thanks to their characteristic bulges at the rooftop. Pennsy acquired 52 of the 948 GP30's outshopped by EMD, putting them in the EF group as EF22's (EMD freight, 2,250 hp.). GP30 No. 2219 is first out on a three-unit combination that includes two General Electric U25B's (PRR Class GF25). This is westbound freight NWC-1 along the Susquehanna River near Duncannon, Pa., on June 10, 1965. *Robert Malinoski*

buy a set of EMD E7 passenger diesels (originally Class EP3, later Class EP20). The streamlined bulldog-nose units were deemed "experimental" and placed in secondary passenger service between Harrisburg and Detroit, ostensibly to please the folks at General Motors. Soon the E7's were catching the eyes of management. These locomotives were outstanding performers. In 1947, the PRR placed an order for more and eventually had a fleet of 59 E7A cabs and E7B boosters and 74 of the E7 successor, the E8 (Class EP22), which it purchased in cab-only form.

CLASS ES: The PRR grouped its various Electro-Motive switchers into the ES class, subgrouping them according to horsepower. PRR owned 237 EMD switchers, purchased between 1937 and 1957; they were used nearly systemwide.

CLASS EF: The once-skeptical Pennsylvania continued to buy EMDs and eventually owned nearly 1,500 diesels in 21 different models. It bought more diesels from EMD than from any other builder! While it missed the rush on Electro-Motive's revolutionary FT models, the PRR did buy 365 F-units of various types, including the FP7 for passenger service. They were purchased between 1947 and 1952, including four

secondhand F3B's from Bangor & Aroostook. All were used systemwide outside electrified lines.

CLASS ERS: When EMD introduced the 1,500-hp GP7 (Class ERS15 and ERS15s) and later the 1,750-hp GP9 (Class ERS17), PRR bought hundreds of these popular EMD "Geeps" between 1952 and 1959. Included were variations such as those equipped with steam generators for passenger service (GP7's only) and cabless GP9's (40 of them, although they did not have their own class) for use as booster units. Because of their versatility, the Geeps could be found throughout the system, on main lines as well as branches, hauling through road freights, podunk way freights and occasionally even named passenger trains. The ERS group also included six-axle versions of of the Geep, EMD models SD7 and SD9, primarily intended for light-railed branch lines with grades.

CLASS EF (SECOND GROUP): This class included many of EMD's "second-generation" road-switchers, most of which were turbocharged. The class included 52 GP30s purchased in 1963; 119 GP35's, 40 SD35's, 65 SD40's, and 65 SD45's purchased in 1964-65; and five non-turbocharged GP38's bought in 1967 for the PRSL.

Fairbanks-Morse

Pennsylvania's fleet of 200 Fairbanks-Morse diesels was the largest fleet of opposed-cylinder diesels in the U.S. The railroad's F-M roster looked like the builders' catalog; PRR owned eight different models, including FM's attractive H10-44 and H12-44 switchers (PRR Class FS10 and FS12 respectively) and its H-series four- and six-axle road-switchers—the FRS class on the PRR—including nine of Fairbanks' landmark 2,400-hp. Train Masters.

The Pennsy F-M roster also featured both varieties of F-M cab units: CF16-4 "C-Liners (PRR Class FF16), and the "Erie-builts" (Class FF20)—so named because the carbodies were built by General Electric at Erie, Pa. The Eries were intended for both passenger and freight service but later regeared for freight service only. Although it was the largest F-M fleet, PRR's F-Ms represented less than 10 percent of its total fleet, and were relatively uncommon on much of the system.

General Electric

CLASS GS4: Prior to GE's entrance into the heavy locomotive market it built several models of lightweight switchers. PRR bought 46 GE 44-tonners between 1948 and 1950. The railroad primarily used the little GE's for waterfront switching on light trackage in New York, Philadelphia, and Baltimore. These small engines were Class GS4, and should never be confused with

Southern Pacific's majestic Lima 4-8-4 *Daylight*s, of the same designation!

GF CLASS: PRR owned relatively few General Electric diesels because GE entered the heavy diesel-electric market only a few years before the Penn Central merger. Nevertheless, PRR did have 59 of GE's pioneering U25B (Class GF25), and 20 of the much rarer six-motor U25C (Class GF25a). It also owned 15 U28C's (Class GF28a) and 5 U30C's (GF30a).

Lima-Hamilton

CLASS SRS25: Not to be forgotten, were PRR's 22 Lima-Hamilton 2,500 hp center-cab transfer locomotives. These were Lima's only transfer locomotives, and PRR's only Lima diesels. Lima-Hamilton only produced diesels for a few years before it merged with Baldwin in 1950. They were used primarily in heavy freight service west of Pittsburgh. 🚂

Dieselization on the PRR had just commenced in a big way when this handsome A-B-A set of Fairbanks-Morse Eries grinding uphill between Horseshoe and Gallitzin with manifest "QD" was captured on film. The units were nearly new, the 36 Erie A units and 12 B units (PRR Class FF20) having been purchased in 1947-48. The photo was taken on July 24, 1948. *Bruce D. Fales, Jay Williams Collection*

The Pennsy owned several ponderous center-cab transfer diesels. Three Baldwin 2,400-hp. RT-624 models (part of PRR's BRS group) move a transfer job through Manayunk in suburban Philadelphia in 1965. The railroad had 22 of these Baldwin center-cabs and 22 similar models from Lima. *John Dziobko*

It's the evening of October 20, 1967, and the Pennsylvania Railroad is just about at the end of its line with less than four months to live. Meanwhile, the *St. Louisan*—at one time a proud liner on the St. Louis-New York run—pauses for non-existent passengers at Effingham, Ill. Two coaches are more than sufficient for tonight's passenger load; most of the train's revenues are coming from the express and mail being carried on its several head-end cars, but even this traffic will continue to decline during the ensuing months. Like the PRR itself, the *St. Louisan* will become history under the Penn Central name. *Tom Hoffmann*

11

Twilight of the Pennsylvania Railroad

DECLINE, MERGER, AND BANKRUPTCY

The Pennsylvania Railroad was one of the largest, most powerful institutions during the first half of the twentieth century. To many people, the PRR was more than just a railroad; it was a way of life. That the mighty PRR would ever consider merging with its arch rival, the New York Central, was simply inconceivable, and that both companies would ultimately fall into bankruptcy was absolutely unimaginable.

The decline of the Pennsylvania Railroad happened gradually during the course of more than 40 years and was the result of many problems, some within the railroad's control, others beyond it. One of its biggest problems was that it suffered from a slow erosion of its traffic base. The heavy "smokestack" industries that once provided the PRR with the lion's share of its freight traffic began to fold and relocate away from the Northeast even before the Great Depression struck. But during the 1930s, many companies closed, never to reopen. Things got worse. Following World War II there was a mass exodus of industry from the Northeast as firms moved south and west. The demand for coal, one of PRR's staple commodities, was in decline as fuel oil began to replace coal as a home heating fuel—and as a way of moving trains. After World War II, there was a series of crippling coal strikes that drove the price up, and demand down.

The PRR had one the most incredible network of passenger routes in the U.S. It moved tens of millions of people annually. But government-sponsored improved highways, mass-produced automobiles, and cheap gasoline encouraged people to drive rather than take the train. This erosion by the automobile began seriously affecting PRR's patronage in the 1920s. Then, in 1930s, air travel began to divert still more railroad passengers. Although World War II briefly reversed the trend, passenger traffic and revenues dropped precipitously again after. The railroad only briefly slowed the loss of its ridership by offering new services and attractive new trains, such as the "Fleet of Modernism" streamlining of 1938 that was applied to the *Broadway Limited*, *Liberty Limited*, and other trains, and such new innovations as the *Aerotrain* of the 1950s. But in the long term these efforts were largely superficial and ineffective. Complicating matters, the government made it very difficult for the railroad to discontinue trains, even when they were running well below capacity

In the 1920s, the same highways which gave rise to the private automobile also served over-the-road trucking companies. Initially the PRR sought to combat this competition with its own trucks, but this was deemed anti-competitive by the Federal government, and the railroad was forced to divest its trucking subsidiary. In the early 1940s, the Pennsylvania Turnpike was begun to connect Philadelphia with Pittsburgh—the heart of PRR's domain. But this was just the beginning of government-

Illustrating the downfall of the PRR is this sad view of a shabby Penn Central *Broadway Limited* being backed into Chicago Union Station for loading on an afternoon in 1970. Somber black has replaced elegant Tuscan red on the locomotives, and PC green has likewise dulled the exteriors of the *Broadway*'s passenger cars. In an equally depressing state, the Pennsy's once-impressive Polk Street Freight Station looms in the background, its once-busy platforms and tracks now perilously empty of freight movement. *Mike Schafer*

financed competition. In 1956, President Dwight Eisenhower initiated the ultimate American road network: the Interstate Highway System. The Federal government spent billions of dollars on these new super roads, providing low-cost "tracks" for trucking companies, and the result for the PRR was increased traffic losses. Now, trucks could provide better, faster service than the railroad in many key city pairs. The PRR, and all other American railroads, were further hampered by strict Federal regulations regarding rate structures. Simply, the railroads were unable to adjust their rates to compete effectively with trucks.

Other problems that affected the industry as a whole hit the PRR especially hard. As their traffic was eroding, many railroads were also pinched by higher labor costs. Railroads were unable to effectively reduce their labor costs because of binding union agreements and inflexible work rules. Even when railroads were faced with an immediate loss of business, they could not drastically cut employment. Since the PRR historically had an enormous labor pool, its labor burden was significantly greater than with smaller carriers.

Although many of these factors lay beyond the Pennsylvania's immediate control, ineptitude on the part of its management did not help matters. In the 1930s, the railroad might have been able to take steps toward stabilizing some problems but failed to recognized the situation until it was too late. By the 1960s, the railroad was in a tailspin from which it was unable to recover. Rather than let its problems become clear to stockholders, the railroad continued to pay dividends and reward

management with bonuses, making up the difference by skimping on maintenance and other vital operations. By 1968, the PRR had more than 700 miles of "slow orders"—speed restrictions—directly attributable to deferred maintenance.

World War II is often viewed as a high point on the PRR and on American railroads in general. During the war, the Pennsy served the nation by carrying unprecedented volumes of freight and passenger traffic. At no time in history had the PRR ever handled so much business, and if the PRR had not been in shape to move this traffic effectively, some historians believe the U.S. may not have been victorious. Yet, the railroad suffered for its heroism. After the war, its motive power was worn out and its infrastructure battered. In 1946, the PRR declared its first loss in history. The writing was on the wall.

A recession swept the nation in 1957, and railroad traffic in the East dropped dramatically. The PRR, which had been watching the slow erosion of its traffic, took a big hit. It sidelined locomotives and furloughed workers. But drastic action was needed. Management recognized then that, unless some radical actions were taken, the "P Company" may not survive.

Railroad consolidation had been discussed since the 1920s as a way of reducing costs and providing better service. Yet, on November 1, 1957, when PRR Chairman James Symes and NYC's Robert Young announced that their railroads were discussing merger, it shocked the business world. All previous discussion of consolidation involved Eastern lines aligning with either the New York Central *or* the PRR. The two companies were age-old foes; how could they seriously consider merger with each other? But that they were.

Before the railroads could come to terms, Young committed suicide. His successor, Alfred Perlman, did not get along well with Symes and the talks fizzled. However, before long the railroads began talking again. NYC was in the same economic situation as the PRR. The two railroad titans hoped that by combining their efforts, they could cut costs and more effectively cope with their real competition: highway transport.

Following several years of negotiations, the two railroads finally agreed to merge by

1965. Meanwhile, Symes retired and was replaced by Stuart Saunders, who came to the PRR from the Norfolk & Western. In 1965, while the merger was pending, the PRR suffered a grave and everlasting lapse in foresight: it tore down Pennsylvania Station in New York—a tragic event, symptomatic of the railroad's deep-seated illness.

The PRR-NYC merger, the largest corporate merger in history, was approved by the Interstate Commerce Commission on April 27, 1966. Many had fought the merger, and it was among the most controversial corporate joinings in U.S. history, but it was a done deal. The two companies were formally merged on February 1, 1968, becoming the Penn Central Transportation Company—the largest transportation company in the world. Its assets were worth nearly $7 billion, and it employed more than 100,000 people. Nevertheless, the merger controversy was justified because PC was one of most badly planned unions in history. Management had devoted all of its efforts pushing the merger through various legal and political obstacles by making concessions to its opponents but gave little thought on how to coordinate the two railroads' operations. There were many serious, unresolved differences between PRR and NYC at the time of the merger.

So, instead of providing the panacea to the railroads' woes, the merger compounded their problems. Where the merger was to have cut costs, its inefficiencies instead increased costs and reduced productivity. One of the great benefits of the merger was to have been significantly reduced labor costs, yet despite a slight cut in its labor pool, PC's labor costs were higher than the two separate railroads before the merger. Further, the chain of command had become blurred; management from both roads had diametrically opposed operating philosophies and fought with each other. The result was utter chaos. Service dropped to an unprecedented low, and the public was outraged. In 1968 PC was losing $400,000 per day. In 1969, PC was forced to take on the ailing New Haven (a condition of the merger), and by year's end PC was losing a half million dollars a day. To make up its deficit, PC borrowed vast sums. But after two years the railroad was sunk. PC declared bankruptcy on June 1, 1970. And, at that time, the railroad was losing more than $800,000 per day. But things got even worse.

Soon Penn Central was joined by a host of other failing Eastern carriers. Many feared a wholesale industry collapse. So, the Federal government stepped in and relieved the railroads of intercity passenger service by creating Amtrak. Since PC operated nearly two-thirds of all intercity passenger trains, this move was specifically aimed at helping the black giant back on its feet. Yet, this was too little too late. To revive PC, and the other failing lines, more drastic measures were needed. The result was a government-sponsored Northeast railroad bailout. On April 1, 1976, PC along with the Reading, Lehigh Valley, Central Railroad of New Jersey, Erie Lackawanna, and several smaller carriers were merged together into a giant new railroad called the Consolidated Rail Corporation—Conrail. In the process, ownership of PC's high-speed, Boston-Washington corridor was transferred to Amtrak.

But, freight traffic was still declining and was yet to hit bottom. However, after the influx of several billions in Federal tax dollars, draconian route divestment and abandonments, and further initiative toward railroad deregulation (culminating with the Staggers Act in 1980), Conrail was finally able to reverse the decline. Slowly, under the skilled management of Stanley Crane, Conrail rebuilt its foundations, and its traffic (and revenues) started to grow. By the mid 1980s, Conrail was showing a profit, and the government returned the railroad to the private sector. Ten years later (as this is being written) Conrail's two primary rail competitors, Norfolk Southern and CSX, were engaged in a bidding war for the now profitable blue giant. As this books goes to press, NS and CSX are set to split up Conrail, with NS acquiring most former-PRR trackage. 🚋

A Penn Central suburban train saddles up to the lonely upper-level platforms of Philadelphia's Thirtieth Street Station in 1974. Although New York's Pennsylvania Station was a casualty of PRR's fall from grace (PRR sold the air rights over the station in a desperate attempt to raise cash), stately Thirtieth Street was a survivor. After undergoing extensive rehabilitation in the 1980s and 1990s, complete with the revival of PRR-style signage and other touches to commemorate the PRR, Thirtieth Street Station today is a proud and busy reminder of the late, great Pennsylvania Railroad. *Mike Schafer*

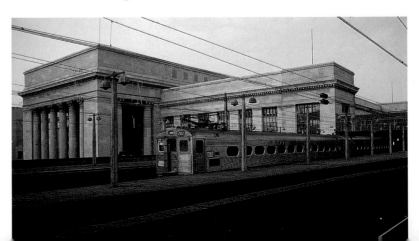

One of the Pennsylvania Railroad's most well-known landmarks—Horseshoe Curve—remains a popular train-watching location, thanks in part of the State of Pennsylvania's redevelopment of Horseshoe Curve Park during the early 1990s. Today the location enjoys historic status, and its new facilities, including a funicular railway that makes the track-level area of the park accessible to everybody (prior to that, a hefty climb up a formidable number of stairs was required by anyone who wanted to watch trains). Conrail has reduced the number of mainline tracks from four to three, but traffic remains dense and still includes helper-locomotive movements and the passenger trains of Amtrak. In this eastward view from July 1988, a Conrail van train sweeps around the Curve on its climb to Gallitzin. The upper park area, with a pseudo Pennsy diesel on display (having replaced the K4s that had been on display for many years before it was restored to operating condition earlier in the 1980s), is visible at right. Today it has been fenced to protect the numerous visitors from venturing into the track area. *Brian Solomon*

The PRR Today

WHERE YOU CAN STILL SEE THE PENNSY

Today, portions of the former Pennsylvania Railroad survive as vital active railroad main lines, but these lines serve dozens of different carriers and passenger agencies, rather then one cohesive railroad. Yet, the mileage of PRR's routes has been greatly trimmed in the nearly 30 years since the railroad's demise. PRR's route structure was first melded with that of the New York Central and then New Haven, followed by the railroads that formed Conrail in 1976. In the process, segments of all the railroads were abandoned, and consolidated. Since the time of the Penn Central merger many of PRR's branches and secondary main lines have fallen into disuse, and many abandoned. A number of its main lines have also been abandoned or downgraded to branch lines. East of Pittsburgh, the PRR has fared reasonably, but west it has not.

Lines East

The former PRR main line east of the sprawling Conway Yard, near Pittsburgh, is one of Conrail's principal routes. Although the historic four-track Main Line has been reduced to two and three tracks in most places, as many as 50 freight trains per day ply former PRR rails between Pittsburgh and Harrisburg. Famous Horseshoe Curve is still a great place to watch the railroad. East of Harrisburg to Philadelphia, the PRR main is primarily a passenger line. Most freight to Philadelphia and the New York area now moves over a combination of former Reading, Lehigh Valley, and Jersey Central routes.

The Northeast Corridor between New York and Washington is the busiest and fastest passenger route in North America. Dozens of Amtrak trains, and hundreds of commuter trains formerly run by PRR and now largely operated by New Jersey Transit, Southeastern Pennsylvania Transportation Authority (SEPTA), and MARC (Maryland Rail Commuter), zip along daily under the wires that the PRR strung in the 1930s. Most of PRR's electrified commuter branches are also busy with passenger traffic. However, changes in traffic patterns have resulted in Conrail discontinuing its former-PRR electric freight operations.

During the last 20 years, Conrail has pruned the former PRR system, selling off branches and secondary lines. This process continues, and even trunk routes such as its Buffalo line via Keating Summit are for sale. Some well-worn PRR routes in the East have not done well. The Elmira branch to Lake Ontario, once a vital coal corridor, was downgraded following the PC merger and was mostly abandoned, although short segments in New York State are operated by short lines. PRR's former New Portage route west of Hollidaysburg over the Muleshoe Curve was abandoned shortly after the Conrail merger.

In the East, many former PRR shops and yards remain active. The shops at Altoona and Hollidaysburg are active facilities; both are crucial to Conrail's operation. Likewise, one of Amtrak's primary facilities is the shop at Wilmington, Del. Sunnyside Yard in Queens is still a busy facility, storing trains for Amtrak, NJ Transit, and Metro-North's Long Island Rail Road between rush hours; and Conway Yard, west of Pittsburgh, is one of Conrail's largest, most important freight facilities.

When the PRR built something, it was intended to be around forever. Witness the bas-relief keystones on the overpass on the Lincoln Highway at Valparaiso, Ind., in 1990. Meanwhile, Amtrak's *Broadway Limited* heads for Chicago. *Mike Schafer* BELOW: PRR's New York-Washington mainline has turned into a high-speed passenger corridor. Note the former-PRR caboose trailing the train at right in this 1992 scene at Newark, Del. *Brian Solomon*

Lines West

The former PRR west of Pittsburgh has been largely fragmented, downgraded, and in many cases abandoned. Following the Penn Central merger, many PRR routes were sacrificed in favor of New York Central lines. The NYC had aggressively modernized its entire plant beginning in 1920s, while the PRR had concentrated primarily on its Eastern routes. By the 1960s, the NYC was a progressive modern railroad, while the PRR had become a rolling museum. Where the Central had installed modern signaling systems and Centralized Traffic Control—enabling dispatchers to remotely authorize train movements by controlling signals through pushbutton controls—the PRR was stilling using antique manual interlocking towers; traditional, directional double track; automatic block signals; and hand-written train orders. Furthermore, the PRR's tracks were badly maintained, and were largely equipped with jointed rail rather than continuous welded rail. Since the two railroads had parallel lines throughout Ohio, Indiana and Illinois, rationalization was easily accomplished by abandoning or downgrading inferior routes and moving all through traffic to the superior route. Today most Conrail traffic uses former New York Central lines.

PRR's old Pittsburgh, Fort Wayne & Chicago is one of the most intact, and one of the more heavily used former PRR Midwestern routes, although traffic on this line tapers off west of Crestline, Ohio. Conrail owns and operates the line from Pittsburgh to Fort Wayne; from Fort Wayne to roughly Gary, Ind., Norfolk Southern operates it. It is mostly abandoned the short distance between Gary and Hammond, but west of there Conrail and Amtrak use the last lap to Chicago as a main line.

The western leg of the Fort Wayne is only one of several parts of the former PRR, now operated by Norfolk Southern. Since the PRR and NS predecessor, Norfolk & Western, had close corporate connections, the NS was a logical successor to some PRR's routes. In 1964, as part of the N&W, Nickel Plate, and Wabash consolidation, the N&W picked up PRR's Columbus-Sandusky line. In more recent times, NS purchased the former PRR line from Cincin-

nati to Richmond, Ind., and from Richmond to New Castle, Ind.

PRR's former route to Cleveland prospered in recent times at the expense of most of PRR's other Midwestern routes. Under the PRR this line was primarily an ore branch; today it serves Conrail and Amtrak as a Pittsburgh-Cleveland connection to the former NYC main; some 20-40 freights a day use the line. Another surviving line is part of the old PRR main to St. Louis, west of Terre Haute, Ind. This line handles a considerable volume of traffic although it has been single-tracked.

Here and there other short segments of the PRR were retained by Conrail as its main line. However, many of PRR's lines were abandoned; including most of the Panhandle line west of Columbus, the majority of PRR's lines to Toledo, Detroit, and between Xenia and Cincinnati, Ohio.

Short lines have picked up many segments. The Ohio Central operates a portion of the Panhandle west of Mingo Junction, Ohio, to Columbus. The Indiana Southern runs part of the line from Indianapolis toward Vincennes, and the Louisville & Indianapolis operates the former PRR between those two cities.

Preservation

The PRR actively preserved examples of its steam and electric power, and as a result Pennsy power is well represented in museums today. The best place to see PRR locomotives is the Railroad Museum of Pennsylvania at Strasburg—one of the finest railroad museums in the U.S.—which has beautifully restored many priceless PRR locomotives. A number of PRR structures have been saved and preserved as well. Some, such as Pennsylvania Station in Baltimore, are still active thriving parts of the railroad. Others, such as Hunt Tower in Huntingdon, Pa., are just museums. There are many sites on the old PRR worth visiting including Horseshoe Curve and the Railroaders' Memorial Museum in Altoona, Washington (D.C.) Union Station, and Thirtieth Street Station in Philadelphia.

Although the PRR has long since faded from the scene, heavy trains still roll along the Juniata River and over the Rockville Bridge; and passengers still ride at speed over the Northeast Corridor and through the tunnels below the Hudson. These portions of railroad that were the PRR will continue to play a vital role for a great many years to come.

Index